ACCESSIBILITY

ACCESSIBILITY

A Transformative Guide of Self-Discovery and Personal Empowerment

Dr. *A*. Romani

Authored Pages
Mt. Prospect, Il USA | (888) 821-3271 | AuthoredPages.com

Published by: **Dr. A. Romani** / Authored Pages
ISBN: 978-1-970666-04-5

"ACCESSIBILITY: A Transformative Guide of Self-Discovery and Personal Empowerment"

ISBN: 978-1-970666-04-5 (print, paperback, PB)
ISBN: 978-1-970666-05-2 (EPUB)

Library of Congress Control Number 2025926396

BISAC: SEL027000 | OCC010000 | PHI006000

Disclaimer: The information in this book is provided for general information only and does not constitute professional advice including but not limited to medical, legal, investment, or financial advice. Always seek professional advice before making important decisions.

DEDICATION

I dedicate this guide to all those who choose to take the next step in their lives to transform themselves into something truly wonderful. This my friends, is your guide and your opportunity to take control. Enjoy the journey, it can seem like a long one but your best is still to come.

TABLE OF CONTENT

INTRODUCTION

In the midst of an ever-evolving world, many individuals find themselves grappling with feelings of inertia, disconnection, and a yearning for something more profound. Your presence here signifies a desire to unravel these complexities and embark on a transformative journey toward self-discovery and empowerment.

This book is designed as a companion for those who seek not only to explore existential themes but also to embrace their truest, most authentic selves. No prior philosophical knowledge or spiritual expertise is necessary to embark on the journey laid out here. All that is required is a willingness to engage with the themes of self-reflection, challenge existing perceptions, and explore new possibilities.

Whether you have a background in existential literature or you are new to personal development, the concepts and strategies offered within these pages are accessible and designed to resonate with anyone committed to enhancing their life experience.

As you embark on this journey, prepare to delve into the essence of who you are and what it means to live an authentic life. Through carefully curated narratives and practical strategies, you will learn to develop mindfulness as a means to cultivate inner peace and clarity. Techniques for embodying your true feelings and desires will gradually reshape how you perceive and interact with the world around you. By confronting limiting beliefs and embracing a mindset predisposed to growth, you will find yourself better equipped to redefine success on your own terms.

You will develop resilience, foster emotional intelligence, and discover the importance of nurturing a supportive network that encourages personal growth. On completion of this book, you will have the tools and mindset necessary to embrace change confidently, set long-term goals, and inspire others by sharing your authentic story. This journey promises to be deeply personal and profoundly rewarding. By the end, you will not only emerge with a greater understanding of your inner force but also with a concrete path to sustained personal growth. Your journey awaits.

DESCRIPTION

Have you ever felt disconnected from the life you're living, as if something vital is missing? This compelling journey, "**ACCESSIBILITY**" invites you to explore the profound questions of existence and the essence of your true self. Guided through a thoughtfully structured path, you'll navigate the complexities of identity, purpose, and emotional freedom with clarity and compassion. Each chapter offers practical tools and insightful reflections designed to help you cultivate mindfulness, embrace vulnerability, and overcome limiting beliefs. Through "**ACCESSIBILITY**" Learn how to harmonize your mind and body, harness the power of intuition, and build resilience that empowers you to face life's challenges with grace. From setting meaningful goals to fostering authentic connections, this experience transcends theory—it becomes a living practice.

CHAPTER 1: The Quest for Authenticity

Understanding Your Identity

Exploring the concept of identity requires delving into a rich tapestry of individual and collective elements that shape who we are. It's a multifaceted construct, encompassing individual attributes, relational dynamics, and broader social affiliations. At its core, individual identity reflects our values, beliefs, and personal traits that define us uniquely. It includes the things you value the most, your personality characteristics, and often manifests in your passions and pursuits. In contrast, relational identity is shaped by the roles you play in the context of others, such as being a parent, sibling, colleague, or friend. These roles are critical in forming our social perceptions and are dynamic, changing with time and experience. The collective identity, meanwhile, involves broader affiliations such as cultural, religious, or professional communities, reflecting a shared sense of belonging that ties individuals to the larger societal fabric.

The quest for authenticity is fundamentally linked to understanding these components of our identity.

Authenticity is about aligning our internal self-concept with our external expressions and experiences. In modern times, particularly as personal well-being gains prominence, embracing authenticity is increasingly recognized as essential for leading a fulfilling life. People experience greater job satisfaction, improved relationships, and enhanced productivity when they live authentically. When individuals live incongruently with their core values and true selves, it often results in dissatisfaction, stress, and a fractured sense of well-being.

In the current era, a significant emphasis is placed on personal growth and mindfulness as pathways to authenticity. Practices that cultivate mindfulness—such as meditation, reflective journaling, and self-reflection—play a critical role in nurturing self-awareness. These practices enable individuals to reconnect with their authentic selves, fostering an environment where self-acceptance and authenticity can flourish. In *2025*, the growing awareness around mindfulness acts as a catalyst for individuals striving to understand and embrace their true identity, free from the shadows of societal expectations and self-imposed limitations.

Understanding one's identity is also deeply intertwined with finding the right alignment in professional and personal spaces. In the workplace, this means seeking environments that resonate with personal values and allow for authentic expression. Job satisfaction is highly contingent upon this alignment, and when individuals find roles or workplaces that fit their identity, it translates into higher engagement and satisfaction levels. Authenticity in the workplace is no longer a luxury but a necessity for holistic well-being. As organizations increasingly recognize the value of diversity and individual expression, this trend is becoming more pronounced.

Within the broader societal framework, the concept of authenticity extends to branding and personal identity in digital spaces. In *2025*, branding—whether personal or professional—places a strong emphasis on authenticity, purpose, and personalization. Brands that foster genuine connections and articulate a clear sense of purpose resonate with audiences that yearn for meaning in their interactions. This broader impersonal emphasis on authenticity mirrors the internal journey of self-discovery that many individuals undertake. In building personal brands, whether through professional networks or social media, the trend towards genuine and meaningful connections underlines the importance of authenticity. Another layer to consider in understanding identity today is the intersection with emerging technologies, particularly in the realm of digital identity and privacy.

The advancement in biometrics and post-quantum cryptography presents new possibilities and challenges. These technologies can enhance the capacity to present a digital identity that is congruent with real-life authenticity. However, they also pose important questions about privacy and how digital representations can either support or hinder one's quest for authenticity. Ensuring that the digital self we project aligns with our true identity becomes increasingly relevant in an age where online interactions are pervasive.

As you embark on this journey within the realm of authenticity and personal identity, acknowledging these multifaceted components is critical. Each layer of identity holds the potential to either empower or constrain, based on how well it aligns with your true self. By adopting practices that foster self-awareness and aligning your roles and affiliations with your core values, you can pave the way towards a more authentic existence. This alignment brings about a transformative change in how you perceive yourself and how you are perceived by others.

The pursuit of authenticity is progressive and iterative. It involves continuous refinement and re-evaluation as life circumstances shift and new experiences are encountered. It involves letting go of misconceptions and outdated roles that no longer serve you, making space for growth and new identities to emerge. This continuous evolution is both a challenge and an opportunity, offering possibilities to expand and deepen your understanding of self.

At the heart of this journey is the recognition that authenticity is not a state of being but a continuous practice. It requires courage and vulnerability to express your true self in a world that often values conformity over individuality. The reward is a richer, more meaningful life, characterized by a genuine sense of connection with oneself and others. Individual and collective identities, when harmoniously integrated, foster resilience and empower you to navigate life with clarity and purpose.

Embracing authenticity and understanding identity are not mere personal endeavors but ripple out to influence societal structures and interactions. When individuals are true to themselves, they contribute to a more transparent and authentic society, bridging gaps between diverse perspectives and values.

The insights garnered from this quest for authenticity have the power to transform personal realities and inspire change in the world around you. This exploration of identity is an invitation to explore deeply, engage with diverse facets of yourself, and embark upon an evolutionary path of self-discovery and personal empowerment. It is a profound quest to be embraced with openness and curiosity, a true alignment with the essence of who you are. As you venture through this landscape, remember that understanding your identity is the cornerstone of living authentically and unlocking the deeper potentials within you.

Navigating Societal Expectations

In a world where societal expectations persistently shape our daily lives, many find themselves grappling with a profound quest for authenticity. These expectations manifest in various forms, from imposed gender roles and career milestones to broader cultural pressures, each contributing to a sometimes invisible yet palpable guide for how life should unfold. For many, particularly women and marginalized communities, these expectations can feel restrictive, trapping them in paradigms that may not resonate with their core identities. As individuals strive to meet these societal markers, such as career advancement or familial roles, they may encounter a discord between external successes and internal fulfillment. This dissonance often leads to feelings of emptiness and disconnection, as the chase for externally defined success can overshadow personal truth and authenticity.

Navigating these societal expectations requires confronting the pressure to conform while remaining true to oneself. The balance between authenticity and conformity is a delicate negotiation, where one strives to align external actions with internal convictions. This requires a conscious effort to understand and articulate personal values, enabling mindful decision-making that respects both individual integrity and societal relationships. For many, this involves a continuous practice of self-reflection—a process that goes beyond self-actualization as envisioned by Abraham Maslow. Self-actualization, rather than a static endpoint, is an evolving journey. It encompasses an understanding of one's potential, the alignment of one's life with core values, and the intentional pursuit of purpose. This path demands constant introspection and the courage to make choices that genuinely reflect one's beliefs and goals, even in the face of societal pressures.

Authenticity becomes more than just a personal preference; it is a necessary element for resilience, particularly for those who navigate discriminatory environments. For marginalized groups, such as LGBTQ+ youth, embracing authenticity is a profound act of self-preservation. It allows for the creation of identity spaces where they can thrive despite external adversities. These individuals often face societal expectations that conflict with their identities, and as such, authenticity serves as a powerful means to resist and transform these pressures. It becomes a beacon for empowerment, fostering communities that celebrate rather than suppress individuality.

The pursuit of authenticity in the face of societal expectations is complicated by the rapidly evolving landscape of technology. Today, voices are raised about the impact of artificial intelligence on genuine expression. A generational divide has emerged, influencing perceptions of authenticity. Younger generations often place greater value on the intention and emotional impact behind communication rather than its origin. In contrast, some view AI involvement in personal expression as inherently detracting from authenticity. Authenticity is increasingly seen as multi-dimensional, shaped by intent, emotional investment, and the dynamic interplay between human expression and technological enhancement. These evolving perceptions challenge the traditional understanding of authenticity, pushing individuals to reconsider how they articulate truth in a technologically mediated world.

As the discourse on authenticity progresses, a broader societal shift towards purpose-driven living and marketing emerges. In *2025*, individuals and brands alike are called to align more closely with authentic values and purposes. This movement underscores the importance of integrating authenticity into both personal and professional realms. It suggests that genuine connections, forged through shared ideals and honest interactions, are increasingly valued over superficial exchanges. In this climate, aligning personal pursuits and professional ventures with true values not only paves the way for individual fulfillment but also cultivates an environment where others are inspired to seek their own truth.

The pressures to conform can obscure the path to authenticity, making it essential to develop strategies that help navigate societal expectations without losing sight of the self. One effective approach is to cultivate a practice of regular self-reflection. This involves setting aside time to reflect on personal experiences, values, and aspirations, examining the alignment between them and one's daily actions. By doing so, individuals can become more aware of discrepancies between society's demands and their authentic desires, enabling adjustments that honor both personal integrity and necessary social engagement.

Building a support network is vital for those traversing the terrain of societal expectations and authenticity. Engaging with like-minded individuals who share similar values can provide affirmation and encouragement, reinforcing resilience in the face of external pressures. Such communities can offer both perspectives and solidarity, empowering individuals to express their uniqueness while navigating societal landscapes that may not always be welcoming.

The challenge extends to recognizing and articulating personal values that truly resonate within. Understanding what is important and defining success and meaning in personal terms provides a foundation from which authentic decisions can be made. This clarity can guide interactions with societal constructs, allowing individuals to engage selectively and thoughtfully with expectations that align with their genuine selves. Ultimately, navigating societal expectations in the quest for authenticity is about finding harmony between external pressures and internal truths. It's about fostering a life where one's actions consistently reflect deeper principles, cultivating a sense of peace and fulfillment that transcends external validation.

As technology continues to shape societal norms, and as perceptions of authenticity evolve, the need for intentional living becomes more pronounced. The journey to authenticity, while complex, is rewarding as it unfolds a life enriched by self-expression. purpose and articulate Being authentic in a world with preset roles demands bravery and constant perseverance.

It implores individuals to break free from the confines of societal norms and to engage thoughtfully with their sense of identity. Navigating societal expectations is not merely about resisting conformity but engaging in a transformative dialogue with it. When authenticity is embraced fully, it becomes a driving force of personal growth, illuminating a path towards a life profoundly connected to one's true self and, consequently, to the broader tapestry of human experience.

Finding Your True Voice

In the journey towards authenticity, finding your true voice stands as an essential milestone. It involves a profound process of self-discovery, undertaken to understand the depths of one's character, motivations, and sense of purpose. This journey isn't solely about the audible voice but rather the articulation of your intrinsic values, passions, and beliefs, untainted by societal expectations or external pressures. Self-discovery in this context means peeling back the layers of imposed identities to unearth the core truths that define who you are and what resonates with you most deeply.

Values form the bedrock of your true voice, guiding decisions and providing clarity in times of uncertainty. To discover your true voice, it is paramount to identify what principles are most significant to you. Reflecting on moments that elicit strong emotional responses can be insightful, revealing priorities and values that might have remained obscured by life's busyness. This focus on values aligns actions with your aspirations, ensuring that the life decisions you make resonate with your foundational beliefs.

Recognizing your strengths is another crucial element of this exploration. Understanding your natural abilities and talents allows you to engage with the world authentically. Talents that are leveraged can serve as vehicles for expressing your true voice. This requires an honest appraisal of skills and inclinations, celebrating both innate abilities and those honed over time. This recognition empowers you to pursue paths that not only align with but amplify your inherent capabilities.

Passion is the energy that fuels your true voice. Discovering what activities or causes ignite this passion is a transformative aspect of self-discovery. When engaged in something you are passionate about, your true voice is naturally expressed with enthusiasm and clarity. Identifying these interests involves trial and discovery, embracing curiosity, and allowing yourself to experiment with new ideas and fields. Through this process, you may uncover hidden passions that were previously overshadowed by societal expectations.

Limiting beliefs, those persistent thought patterns that hinder growth, must be identified and confronted. These beliefs, often internalized from external sources, can obscure your true voice with doubts and fears. Recognizing these patterns involves critical self-examination and a willingness to challenge assumptions you hold about yourself. As these limiting beliefs are dismantled, your confidence in expressing your true voice strengthens, paving the way for authentic living.

Authentic expression encompasses finding means to communicate and act in ways that feel genuinely aligned with your inner self. Whether through verbal communication, creative outlets, or professional paths, how you present yourself should reflect your true identity. This authenticity ensures that interactions with the world do not betray your core values and beliefs. Achieving this congruence involves a blend of introspection and active adjustment, consistently aligning your external expressions with your internal convictions.

The psychological framework underpinning these processes is rooted in humanistic psychology. As theorized by Carl Rogers, the alignment between the "ideal self" and the "real self" is crucial for personal growth. This congruence allows individuals to live authentically, experiencing a sense of fulfillment and inner peace.

It fosters an understanding not only of who you are but also of how you wish to engage with the world around you.

Tools such as journaling and reflection become invaluable in this pursuit. Journaling provides a space for authentic expression, enabling you to capture and reflect on thoughts and emotions privately. Regularly engaging in written reflection can reveal patterns and insights, focusing your journey towards uncovering your true voice. Similarly, reflection and introspection invite you to and consider experiences and emotional responses, offering clarity and understanding about your motivations and desires.

Support networks play a pivotal role in this journey. Connecting with others who encourage authenticity provides reassurance and perspective. Friends, mentors, and support groups offer feedback and encouragement, helping you navigate challenges and celebrate milestones. Engaging with these communities fosters a sense of belonging and shared purpose, reinforcing your commitment to uncovering and expressing your true voice.

Through these practices, the benefits of finding your true voice become evident. There is an increased sense of life satisfaction and a more profound connection to purpose. Living authentically allows for conscious decision-making, where actions are informed by self-awareness rather than automatic responses to external pressures. This intentional approach supports a more meaningful and fulfilling life, with each choice reflecting genuine values and aspirations.

In some contexts, such as gender identity, the journey towards finding your true voice encompasses both verbal and non-verbal expressions. It involves understanding how aspects like pitch, vocabulary, and mannerisms contribute to the expression of identity. Adjustments in communication can create spaces where the true self is more accurately represented and understood, fostering an environment for authenticity.

The journey to discovering your true voicc is deeply personal and requires patience and courage. It is a commitment to authenticity in a world that often demands conformity. As you engage with this process, embracing both the challenges and the triumphs, you articulate a life that is truly your own. The power of your true voice lies in its ability to guide, inspire, and connect you with the world in a way that is surely undeniably authentic and profoundly meaningful.

CHAPTER 2: Existential Questions Unveiled

What Does It Mean to Exist?

The question of existence is one that humans have pondered across cultures and centuries. It taps into the very heart of what it means to be human, addressing the fundamental inquiries that define our lives: "Why am I here?" "What is my purpose?" These questions are not just philosophical musings but are deeply woven into the fabric of the human experience, influencing how we perceive our lives, our choices, and our legacy. At its core, the exploration of existence seeks to uncover the meanings and truths that guide us toward an authentic and purposeful life.

Existentialism, a prominent philosophical movement, offers a framework for understanding these inquiries. Emerging in the *19*th and *20*th centuries, existentialism emphasizes the individual's role in creating meaning in a world that inherently lacks it. Søren Kierkegaard, Friedrich Nietzsche, and Jean-Paul Sartre are among the key figures who championed the idea that life does not come pre-packaged with purpose, but rather, it is up to each person to carve their own path and define their own meaning. This philosophy argues that relying solely on external systems, whether religious, cultural, or societal, for a sense of purpose can lead to disillusionment. Instead, existentialism places the burden of freedom on the individual, championing personal responsibility in the quest for authenticity.

Living authentically, according to existentialist thought, means aligning one's actions and decisions with their true self, free from societal masks or imposed roles. It requires an honest assessment of one's values, desires, and inclinations. Authenticity is not a state to be achieved but a continuous practice of self-awareness and intentional living. It involves acknowledging the inevitable human conditions, such as mortality and freedom, and making choices that genuinely reflect personal truths. However, this freedom is accompanied by the anxiety of decision-making, as the responsibility for one's path is undividedly personal.

Existential questions invite us to embrace the notion of personal freedom and responsibility as one of life's core tenets. The freedom to choose our path and define our existence carries with it the weight of responsibility not just for our own lives, but also in consideration of others'. Sartre famously asserted that in choosing for oneself, one is also choosing for all humanity. This interconnectedness suggests that personal choices resonate beyond the individual and contribute to the common fabric of human experience. It highlights the ethical dimension within existentialism, where freedom is balanced by the awareness of one's impacts and obligations to others.

Addressing these profound questions through the lens of positive psychology provides an empowering approach. Positive psychology, rather than fixating on human flaws, encourages the cultivation of strengths, purpose, and well-being. It complements existentialism by focusing on the aspects of life that promote human flourishing. This approach enables individuals to confront existential worries about meaning and purpose in a constructive manner, fostering resilience and personal growth. By harnessing positive emotions, nurturing fulfilling relationships, and engaging in purposeful activities, individuals can navigate existential challenges with grace and develop a life that is not only authentic but also enriched by fulfillment.

The search for meaning and purpose is inherently personal and varies greatly from one individual to the next. Some find meaning through relationships, others in work or creativity, and yet some in contemplation or spirituality. Regardless of the path, the journey toward understanding what lends weight and significance to life is deeply transformative. This exploration can lead to profound personal empowerment and self-discovery, unveiling hidden strengths and forging connections between past aspirations and future possibilities.

Exploring existential questions invites transformative change by confronting life's inevitable uncertainties and embracing them as pathways to growth. Engaging deeply with these questions allows individuals to emerge with a more resilient outlook on life, appreciating the fluidity of existence and the capacity for continual renewal. It is through questioning and reflection that one discovers not fixed answers, but a dynamic understanding of what it means to live fully and authentically.

Existential crises, moments when the questions of existence become particularly poignant and distressing, can be pivot points for transformation. Far from being purely negative, these crises can act as catalysts for profound personal change. By acknowledging these feelings of anxiety or despair, individuals can embark on a journey that fosters deeper self-awareness and integration. In this process, one learns to navigate the paradoxes of life, such as the coexistence of joy and sorrow, certainty and doubt.

The transformative process of engaging with existential questions also builds resilience, equipping individuals with the tools needed to face life's challenges. The resilience developed through existential inquiry does not eliminate adversity but provides a buffer, allowing individuals to adapt and thrive in the face of life's inevitable trials. It fosters a mindset that appreciates life's impermanence and embraces its moments fully, understanding that existence, while transient, offers boundless opportunities for meaning.

As individuals delve into what it means to exist, they craft a narrative that is uniquely their own. This personal narrative provides cohesion and direction, anchoring one in the present while providing a roadmap for the future. It seeks to blend aspirations with realities, dreams with daily life, knitting together the diverse threads of personal experience into a coherent whole. This narrative is not static but evolves, mirroring the ongoing journey of self-discovery and growth.

The exploration of what it means to exist is a profound journey that intertwines self-awareness, choice, responsibility, and transformation. It calls for an earnest engagement with life's most challenging questions, fostering an authentic and enriching existence. It reveals the latent potentials within everyone, the intrinsic capacity for love, creativity, and purpose, guiding them to not just question their existence, but to live it with boldness and authenticity.

Confronting Meaninglessness

The challenge of confronting meaninglessness is a pivotal aspect of existential inquiry, a profound journey into understanding life's purpose—or lack thereof. This quest can lead to a state of existential despair or an awakening to life's profound possibilities. The fear of meaninglessness, central to existential thought, is one of four primary existential concerns proposed by Irvin Yalom, alongside death, freedom, and isolation. These elements form the bedrock of existential anxiety, arising from the notion that without inherent meaning, life may appear void of purpose and direction. This confrontation with the void can feel daunting, yet it opens the door to a deeper understanding of oneself and the world.

Philosophical perspectives vary in their interpretation of life's inherent meaning or lack thereof. Some suggest life is fundamentally meaningless, positing that any significance attributed to it is a human construct. This perspective challenges individuals to take responsibility for crafting their own meaning. In contrast, others contend that life consists of both meaningful and meaningless elements, changing with one's perception and circumstances. This dual view fosters an appreciation for human agency in weaving meaning through life's tapestry, emphasizing personal interpretation and the active pursuit of purpose.

Albert Camus, a pivotal figure in existential philosophy, explored the tension between humanity's desire for meaning and the indifferent universe in which we operate. He described this tension as "the absurd"—a recognition of life's inherent meaninglessness coupled with a relentless quest for significance. Camus proposed a paradigm of active nihilism, which encourages embracing this absurdity and recognizing the freedom it affords. Through acceptance of life's inherent absurdity, individuals can reclaim agency, creating meaning within the limitations of existence. This approach transforms the confrontation with absurdity into an opportunity for self-creation and liberation.

Creating meaning becomes a central task for individuals wrestling with existential meaninglessness. Viktor Frankl's experiences and insights provide a robust framework for this endeavor. Frankl, a psychiatrist and Holocaust survivor, introduced the concept of "logotherapy," which focuses on life's search for meaning as a primary motivational force. He argued that, even amidst suffering, individuals can find meaning through the attitudes they adopt and choices they make. This emphasizes the proactive nature of meaning creation, urging individuals to actively engage with their environment and personal experiences to forge a life imbued with purpose.

Existential therapy offers a practical methodology for addressing meaninglessness. This therapeutic approach draws on the existential philosophies of thinkers such as Søren Kierkegaard, Jean-Paul Sartre, and Martin Heidegger. It encourages clients to delve into their existential concerns, such as fear of death and isolation, to emerge with a clearer understanding of their life's purpose and authenticity. Through this therapeutic process, individuals are guided to confront their innate desire for meaning, fostering a life that aligns with their genuine desires and aspirations. The therapeutic space becomes a realm for exploring values, examining choices, and confronting fears, ultimately leading to an empowered existence.

Personal growth resides at the intersection of confronting meaninglessness and creating meaning. Recognizing the absence of inherent purpose in life not only challenges individuals but also empowers them. This awareness invites a reevaluation of goals and priorities, encouraging a shift from passive existence to active engagement with life's possibilities. By embracing the freedom to choose and create meaning, individuals harness the complexities of human existence to drive personal transformation and fulfillment.

The confrontation with meaninglessness empowers individuals to explore the depths of their inner world, shedding light on hidden potentials and latent desires. It serves as a crucible for identity formation and self-discovery, where individuals question and redefine themselves in the absence of prescribed paths. This can foster resilience, as individuals learn to navigate uncertain and ambiguous terrains with purpose and resolve. The ability to create personal meaning becomes a source of empowerment, enabling individuals to approach life with intention and clarity.

Empowerment through confronting meaninglessness is not merely an intellectual exercise but a holistic engagement with the self and the world. It invites a comprehensive reevaluation of personal values, relationships, and goals, prompting individuals to align their actions with their true essence. This alignment fuels a sense of authenticity and coherence, enriching life with purpose beyond societal or external validations. As individuals engage in this transformative process, they cultivate a renewed appreciation for life's inherent possibilities, generating fulfillment that emanates from within.

Acknowledging and confronting existential meaninglessness is a catalyst for personal empowerment and self-discovery. It calls individuals to participate in the ongoing creation of their life narratives, integrating past experiences, present decisions, and future aspirations into a coherent and meaningful whole. This process is not merely about finding individual purpose but about contributing to the larger human experience, recognizing the interconnectedness of all life and the shared journey of seeking meaning. By embracing this shared human endeavor, individuals find themselves part of a collective quest for authenticity and significance.

Confronting meaninglessness serves as a threshold to deeper existential understanding. It transforms fear into opportunity, despair into creativity, and isolation into connection. As individuals embrace their capacity to create meaning, they embark on a journey of inner exploration that enriches their lives and those they touch. The journey is one of both personal and collective empowerment, celebrating the resilience and creativity inherent in humanity's quest for meaning. Through this exploration, the seemingly daunting landscape of meaninglessness becomes a terrain rich with possibility and potential, awaiting discovery and transformation.

Defining Your Purpose

Defining one's purpose is a central endeavor in the exploration of existential questions, serving as a foundational aspect of personal empowerment and self-discovery. This quest addresses the quintessential questions that have occupied human thought for centuries: "Who am I?" "What is the purpose of my life?" and "How do I make sense of my existence in the face of mortality?" These inquiries cut across cultural, religious, and philosophical boundaries, inviting each person to embark on a personal journey towards meaning and fulfillment.

The pursuit of meaning is considered a primary human drive, a core component of our existence as emphasized by Viktor Frankl through his pioneering work in logotherapy. Frankl's logotherapy, often referred to as "meaning-centered therapy," posits that the search for meaning is more fundamental than the pursuit of pleasure or power. This approach underscores the idea that understanding one's purpose can be a greater source of satisfaction and resilience than any external achievement or possession.

Logotherapy provides insightful tools for addressing existential questions, offering pathways for personal growth and healing. According to this therapeutic approach, even the most challenging circumstances can offer meaning, provided individuals are willing to seek it out. Frankl suggests that finding meaning is achievable through emotional connections, empathy, and cultivating a deep sense for the intrinsic value of experiences. It implies that purpose may be discovered not only in grand life goals but also in everyday moments rich with potential for insight and understanding.

In the quest for meaning, certain conditions can facilitate this discovery, though they are not prerequisites. Many find that a secure and safe physical environment, along with nurturing relationships, create a fertile ground for the exploration of purpose. Nevertheless, Frankl's insights illuminate the capacity to derive meaning even in the absence of these conditions. By honing one's ability to perceive and remain open to life's nuances, meaning can be unearthed in unexpected places and circumstances. This openness fosters a receptivity to life's inherent potential for significance, urging individuals to see beyond the apparent and embrace the deeper essence of their experiences.

Existential concerns often accompany the journey to define purpose, presenting both challenges and opportunities for growth. The burden of choice and the inherent freedom to shape one's own life can indeed be sources of anxiety, as the responsibility to act and make decisions aligns with creating a meaningful existence. Existential isolation, another common concern, underscores the solitary nature of the human experience, yet it also opens pathways to forge meaningful connections that transcend this isolation. In this duality, opportunities arise for profound personal growth and a more nuanced self-awareness.

The process of defining purpose demands practical engagement and reflection on personal values and experiences. Reflection acts as a tool for identifying the elements of life that hold true significance, serving as a compass to navigate the internal landscape. Delving into one's values provides insight into what energizes and motivates, helping to discern the aspects of life that align with one's deepest convictions.

Developing emotional connections and empathy is another means of detecting value and meaning in life. Relationships often reveal multiple facets of our purpose, highlighting how our actions and expressions of care contribute to the world. Empathy fosters an appreciation for the interconnectedness of human experience, guiding individuals to perceive purpose not solely as a personal endeavor but as a shared journey enriched by collective humanity.

Cultivating openness and perception allows recognition of potential meaning in everyday experiences, regardless of their apparent insignificance. The tender moments of life, the subtle engagements with art, nature, or a fleeting interaction, can illuminate the path to purpose when approached with curiosity and attentiveness. Embracing these moments encourages a deeper connection to the present, presenting opportunities for discovery and transformation.

Addressing existential isolation by fostering good relationships and a sense of community contributes significantly to defining one's purpose. Humans are inherently social beings, and building supportive networks creates a context for experiencing purpose through shared goals and mutual support. Community not only mitigates feelings of isolation but also offers a broader canvas on which individuals can paint their purpose, contributing to something greater than themselves.

Defining your purpose in life is an ongoing journey—a dynamic and evolving process rather than a static endpoint. It requires an embrace of uncertainty and the courage to explore uncharted territories within oneself. This journey is marked by both introspective reflection and active participation in the world, where purpose is not only found but continually created. Each decision, interaction, and experience adds to the narrative of one’s existence, crafting a story rich with meaning and aligned with authentic self-understanding.

Realizing and defining a personal purpose involves embracing both the existential unknowns and the profound potential within. It transforms the abstract questions of existence into actionable insights, allowing individuals to live with intentionality. As individuals engage with these existential questions, they unlock pathways to personal empowerment that shape their journey, navigate the complexities of life, and ultimately reflect a life lived in harmony with profound self-discovery.

Through this exploration, individuals come to understand that defining purpose is not simply an individual pursuit but a meaningful engagement with the human condition. It binds the personal journey with collective experience, harmonizing individual aspiration with communal growth.

This understanding enriches life's narrative, fostering a profound feeling of connection and completeness that transcends the mundane and underscores the vibrant, ever-emergent meaning of human existence.

CHAPTER 3: Mindfulness: The Path Within

Practicing Present Awareness

Practicing present awareness is a cornerstone of mindfulness, offering a pathway to personal empowerment and self-discovery. It involves cultivating an acute awareness of the present moment without the burden of judgment. This practice fosters an ability to meet life's experiences as they unfold, promoting a profound sense of presence and connection with oneself and the world. Engaging fully with the current moment can relieve stress, improve emotional health, and significantly contribute to overall well-being.

Mindfulness encourages a break from the habitual autopilot mode many experience in daily life. The relentless pace of modern living often leads to a life marked by distraction and fragmented attention, where past regrets and future anxieties cloud the clarity of the present. Present awareness acts as an antidote to this tendency, anchoring individuals in the now and providing a refuge from the tumult of thoughts and stressors. By focusing intentionally on the present, individuals can cultivate a deeper connection with their experiences, paving the way for a more engaged and fulfilling life.

A simple yet effective mindfulness practice is mindful breathing. This involves focusing attention on the breath, observing the inhale and exhale without attempting to alter it. A mindful breathing exercise can be as brief as two minutes, making it an accessible practice even for the busiest lifestyle. During the exercise, slow and deep breaths activate the parasympathetic nervous system, which helps promote relaxation. This mindful breathing not only provides calm but also strengthens your ability to regain control over reactions during stressful situations. Returning your attention to the breath whenever the mind starts to wander enhances concentration and resilience.

The body scan is another powerful mindfulness practice that can be instrumental in developing present awareness. This exercise involves attentively tuning into physical sensations throughout the body. Participants start by focusing on their breath and then systematically bring attention to various body parts, from the toes to the head. This practice helps individuals tune into their physical state, fostering a sense of connection with their body. By enhancing body awareness, this practice allows for an integrated experience of mind and body, promoting balance and mindfulness in everyday life.

As you might know, scientific research supports the numerous benefits of mindfulness practices such as stress reduction and improved emotional regulation. Engaging in regular mindfulness exercises trains the mind to remain present, effectively enhancing concentration and focus. This enhanced focus allows individuals to tackle tasks with clear intent and presence, reducing mental fatigue. Individuals who regularly practice mindfulness report a greater sense of calm, grounding, and overall well-being, attesting to its efficacy as a tool for mental health and personal development.

The current landscape of mindfulness has expanded, incorporating new perspectives such as the behavior-analytic approach. This perspective emphasizes integrating present-moment awareness into both personal routines and professional settings. By weaving mindfulness into daily activities and responsibilities, individuals can extend the benefits of present awareness beyond personal introspection to every facet of life.

This holistic approach underscores the adaptability and relevance of mindfulness in contemporary contexts, highlighting how mindfulness practices can be seamlessly integrated into work and life.

Accessibility is a crucial aspect of modern mindfulness practices. With techniques designed for ease of use, mindfulness can now be practiced anywhere and at any time, addressing the constraints of modern life. Tools like mobile applications, guided meditations, and quick mindfulness exercises provide flexible options for individuals to incorporate mindfulness into their routines. These accessible practices make it easier for individuals to cultivate present awareness, regardless of their schedule or environment.

Practicing present awareness through mindfulness significantly impacts self-discovery. By attentively observing thoughts, emotions, and physical sensations as they arise, individuals gain insights into their habitual patterns and underlying motivations. This observational stance helps dissolve judgment and allows for an honest appraisal of personal experiences. This self-discovery process can unveil deeper layers of personal identity and purpose, guiding individuals toward a life that reflects their true values and aspirations. Mindfulness and present awareness also contribute to personal empowerment by enhancing emotional regulation.

By creating a space between stimuli and response mindfulness allows individuals to choose their reactions rather than being dictated by automatic responses. This empowerment is particularly valuable in stressful situations, where a calm and measured response can transform outcomes. By practicing mindfulness, individuals develop the fortitude to navigate life's challenges with intention and poise, resulting in more mindful decision-making.

Living an intentional life, guided by present awareness, offers liberation from the disorientation of life's frenetic pace. This intentionality stems from a grounded mind that exercises clarity and compassion, paving the way for ethical and conscious decisions. With this awareness, actions are not reactionary but deliberate, fostering a life aligned with personal visions and desires.

Embracing present awareness requires commitment and practice, gradually becoming an integral part of one's lifestyle. Starting with short, manageable sessions of mindful breathing or body scanning can lay the foundation for deeper practices. As confidence and comfort with these exercises grow, they embed themselves into daily life, offering benefits that resonate across all domains.

Ultimately, the practice of present awareness through mindfulness empowers individuals to- 44 transform their internal landscapes. It illuminates the path of self-discovery and fosters the ability to live with intention and authenticity. By regularly inviting mindfulness into life, individuals unlock a transformative force, awakening a state of being that harmonizes inner truths with outer realities. As this practice deepens, it invites a richer understanding of life’s tapestry, fostering an enduring peace and connection that nurtures both self and others.

Cultivating Inner Peace

Cultivating inner peace is an integral part of the journey towards mindfulness, serving as a sanctuary amid life's chaos and unpredictability. This practice involves learning to center oneself, allowing a sense of tranquility and calm to permeate both the mind and body. As society accelerates and demands grow, the quest for inner peace becomes not just an aspiration, but a necessity. This is where mindfulness, with its array of techniques and practices, offers tangible pathways to achieving a more serene and balanced state of being.

Mindfulness meditation stands out as an effective practice for nurturing inner peace. This practice involves focusing the mind on the present moment, gently steering awareness away from the ruminations of the past or anxieties about the future. Engaging in guided meditations, even those as brief as ten minutes, can significantly alleviate stress and invoke a sense of calm. Meditation fosters inner stillness, enabling individuals to reconnect with their essential self amidst the clamor of everyday life. By cultivating awareness, mindfulness meditation serves as a powerful tool for grounding oneself, ultimately leading to a more peaceful internal landscape.

Deep breathing techniques like the *4-7-8* method play a crucial role in promoting relaxation and equanimity. This practice involves inhaling for a count of four, holding the breath for seven counts, and exhaling slowly for eight counts. Such methods are designed to activate the parasympathetic nervous system, which supports relaxation processes. Engaging in these mindful breathing exercises provides a quick and effective way to reset in moments of stress, encouraging calm and resilience by allowing the body to return to a state of balance and peace.

Gratitude journaling can be a transformative method for cultivating a positive mindset and fostering inner peace. By consciously recognizing and recording things you are grateful for, even the small and seemingly insignificant, the focus shifts towards abundance rather than deficiency. This shift nurtures a mindset of appreciation and contentment, reducing stress and promoting overall well-being. Gratitude creates an internal dialogue centered on positive reflections and emotions, which acts as a balm against the turbulence often encountered in daily life.

Practices such as mindful eating and walking meditation further enhance the experience of inner peace by fostering presence and engagement with the present moment. Mindful eating involves savoring each bite with full awareness, noticing textures, flavors, and the nourishment received, which promotes a holistic appreciation for the act of eating. Similarly, walking meditation involves a heightened awareness of each step and the surrounding environment, offering a dynamic form of mindfulness that integrates movement with meditative focus. Both practices encourage a deeper connection with the sensory experiences of life, cultivating a calm and centered state of being.

Micro-practices offer an adaptable approach to incorporating mindfulness into daily life, particularly within a fast-paced, demanding world. Short, deliberate moments of quiet or reflection, such as taking three purposeful breaths or surroundings, pause to observe one's provide opportunities for recalibration. These micro-practices embody the principles of mindfulness in a manageable form, facilitating consistent engagement with the present moment and enhancing one's capacity for inner peace.

Physical activities and self-care practices play significant roles in linking mental and physical well-being. Engaging in activities like yoga or stretching helps release physical tension, aligning the body with the mind in harmony.

These activities enhance bodily awareness and promote relaxation, contributing to the overall goal of inner peace. Establishing a self-care routine that includes regular physical activity allows for a holistic approach to well-being, integrating the mental and physical aspects of health into a cohesive practice. The natural world offers a profound and accessible avenue for enhancing inner peace. Spending time outdoors, even if it is limited, has a calming and rejuvenating effect on the mind and body.

Nature provides an opportunity to immerse oneself in the tranquility of natural settings, fostering a sense of grounding and perspective. This connection with nature helps dissolve the barriers of stress and anxiety, serving as a reminder of life's broader context and encouraging a harmonious state of being.

Cultivating inner peace through mindfulness supports a journey of personal transformation and self-discovery. By focusing on the present instead of dwelling on the past or worrying about the future, individuals open themselves to the potential for growth and profound self-awareness. This transformation encourages a deeper understanding of one's values and emotions, fostering empowerment in making choices aligned with authentic desires and intentions.

Current trends highlight the increasing relevance of integrating mindfulness practices seamlessly into everyday routines, ensuring they are accessible and manageable amidst life's complexities. Recognizing the importance of combining mental and physical well-being practices further supports individuals on their journey to inner peace. Techniques like deep breathing, yoga, and mindfulness exercises contribute to a comprehensive strategy for enhancing tranquility and resilience in both mind and body.

The pursuit of inner peace is intrinsically tied to the awakening of personal strength and resilience. This awakening is facilitated through the consistent practice of mindfulness, where individuals learn to navigate life with clarity and confidence. The journey towards inner peace is not about eradicating all stress or conflict but cultivating the capacity to face life's challenges with equanimity and poise.

Through mindfulness, individuals discover that inner peace is not a distant destination but a living, breathing state of being that can be accessed and nurtured daily. It serves as an anchor during turbulent times, offering calm and balance, and helping cultivate a life filled with purpose and joy. As individuals delve deeper into mindfulness, they unlock a reservoir of inner peace that guides them through the tempests of life, illuminating the path to a more compassionate and empowered existence.

Creating a Mindful Routine

Cultivating a mindful routine is an invitation to infuse presence and intention into everyday life. By thoughtfully crafting these routines, individuals can build a sanctuary where stress is mitigated, focus is honed, and self-awareness blossoms. Mindfulness, at its core, is about fully engaging with what is happening in the present moment, and embedding this attention into daily life requires both structure and spontaneity.

Integrating mindfulness techniques into everyday routines begins with small, deliberate steps. Regular meditation or deep breathing exercises are foundational practices that reduce stress and enhance focus. These exercises do not need to be lengthy; even a few minutes each day can significantly impact mental well-being. The regularity of practice solidifies mental clarity and calm, empowering individuals to tackle life's complexities with greater ease.

Simple mindfulness routines, such as gratitude journaling, subtly shift awareness towards positivity and appreciation. By noting daily blessings or moments of joy, individuals train their attention on the abundance in their lives, rather than on challenges. This practice can transform one's perspective, cultivating a mindset of gratitude that endures beyond fleeting moods or circumstances. Gratitude journaling serves as a powerful tool to redirect attention and cultivate a positive mindset.

A dedicated mindfulness space within the home can reinforce the sanctity and continuity of practice. Establishing a corner with calming elements—like soft pillows, gentle lighting, and nurturing plants—creates an inviting retreat for reflection, meditation, and mindfulness activities. This space becomes a physical manifestation of inner peace, offering solace and continuity amid the hustle and bustle of everyday life. It acts as a reminder to embrace stillness and provides an environment conducive to mindful activities, where one can engage in practices like guided meditation or even mindful coloring.

Mindful movement practices further enhance this holistic approach to mindfulness. Activities such as mindful walking, beginner yoga, and balance exercises integrate physical movement with mental awareness. These practices invite participants to connect deeply with their bodies, promoting a harmonious blend of mental clarity and physical vitality. For instance, mindful walking—where attention is brought to the rhythm of the breath, the sensation of the feet on the ground, and the surrounding environment—elevates walking from a mere physical activity to a meditative exercise, nurturing both the body and the mind.

The importance of consistency in mindfulness routines cannot be overstressed. Beginning with one or two practices and gradually expanding them helps maintain motivation and depth. Consistency, not complexity, allows mindfulness to permeate life fully. Mindfulness is about showing up in small, intentional ways rather than striving for perfection in practice. It is a journey that evolves with time, leaving room for adaptation and growth.

The holistic benefits of establishing a mindful routine ripple throughout life. These practices reduce stress, foster deeper concentration, improve physical fitness and posture, and deepen the connection with one's body and environment. Furthermore, they set a solid foundation for personal empowerment and self-discovery, encouraging individuals to engage with life more fully and meaningfully. By nurturing a mindful routine, individuals can transform their relationship with themselves and their surroundings, cultivating a lifestyle imbued with purpose and intention.

Establishing and nurturing a mindful routine requires dedication and the courage to embark on a transformative path. In doing so, individuals navigate toward a more fulfilled and centered life. Over time, these practices sculpt a resilient mindset that embraces the present moment with grace and clarity, enriching every aspect of life. As routines evolve, they continue to offer grounding and insight, illuminating the path to personal empowerment and self-discovery.

Incorporating these practices into daily life allows individuals to explore the depths of their inner world while maintaining a balanced connection with the external world. Through mindfulness, life moves from something passively experienced to something intentionally lived, where every moment is an opportunity for reflection and growth. Over time, these practices foster a profound appreciation for the simple yet profound moments of life and nurture a heart attuned to peace and resilience.

Ultimately, creating a mindful routine is a deeply personal endeavor, shaped by individual needs and aspirations. It's about crafting a ritualistic space that honors life's intricate dance of stillness and movement. Such routines become a means to engage with life's mysteries, challenges, and joys, keeping the spirit of mindfulness alive and vibrant.

Engaging fully with these practices opens the door to personal insight, appreciation, and transformation, offering a timeless gift of inner harmony. Through mindfulness, individuals unlock a framework of consciousness that reverberates throughout their lived experience, leaving a lasting impact on both themselves and the world around them.

CHAPTER 4: Embodiment: Connecting Within

The Power of Body Awareness

The power of body awareness lies at the heart of the journey toward embodiment and personal empowerment. By cultivating an acute sense of body awareness, individuals are invited to deepen their connection with both their physical and emotional states, bridging the often-disconnected realms of body and mind. This heightened awareness provides a gateway to a more holistic experience of life, where mind-body integration fosters greater well-being and personal fulfillment.

One of the most immediate benefits of enhanced body awareness is improved balance and stability. When individuals are attuned to their bodies, they can more effectively coordinate movement, enhancing physical performance and reducing susceptibility to injury. This keen awareness not only aids in physical endeavors but also translates into more nuanced control over one's bodily presence, affecting everything from posture to daily functionality. As individuals learn to navigate their spaces with grace and precision, they cultivate a sense of confidence and competence that supports overall well-being.

Body awareness also plays a significant role in weight management by enabling individuals to recognize and respond effectively to bodily cues such as hunger and fullness. This keen sense of inner awareness aids in distinguishing between eating out of physical necessity versus emotional compulsion. Such clarity can prevent overeating and promote better dietary choices, reducing the risk of obesity and contributing to a healthier lifestyle. By tuning into the body's natural rhythms and signals, one can cultivate an intuitive approach to nourishment that aligns with their health goals.

For those dealing with chronic pain, mindful body awareness presents a potentially transformative approach to pain management. By increasing awareness of bodily sensations, individuals can cultivate greater acceptance and intimacy with their physical selves, which can mitigate the subjective experience of pain. This awareness encourages a shift in focus from suffering to acceptance, empowering individuals to foster resilience and vitality even in the face of discomfort. By deepening the connection with their bodies, individuals can gain insights into their experiences, facilitating a path to healing and well-being.

Enhanced body awareness is also essential in identifying and meeting both physical and emotional needs. By being in tune with bodily cues, individuals can discern between various types of needs—whether it's hunger, thirst, fatigue, or emotional distress—leading to better self-care and emotional satisfaction. This understanding allows for proactive management of one's health and emotional state, reinforcing the capacity for self-regulation and balance. Meeting these needs effectively contributes to a sustained state of well-being.

The mental and emotional benefits of body awareness are equally profound. By promoting balance within the proprioceptive and vestibular systems, body awareness aids in managing stress and anxiety, contributing to a more centered and peaceful state of mind. It reduces the impact of mental health issues such as depression by fostering a healthier mind-body connection. This integration enhances self-awareness, confidence, and emotional stability, all of which are essential for nurturing healthy relationships with both oneself and others.

Recent developments in the study of mind-body interventions highlight their role in increasing body awareness and overall well-being. Practices such as mindfulness and proprioceptive exercises are increasingly recognized as effective tools for harnessing the power of body awareness. By emphasizing the synchronization of mind and body, these interventions offer pathways to holistic wellness, where physical, emotional, and mental health are inextricably linked. The discipline required by these practices reinforces the understanding of one's capabilities, offering insights that extend beyond the immediate physical realm.

In practical terms, cultivating body awareness can significantly enhance motor skills, agility, and coordination. This mastery not only benefits athletic pursuits but also enriches everyday experiences by empowering individuals to move through life with grace and fluidity. Enhanced motor skills contribute to a sense of empowerment stemming from the realization of one's physical potential and ability to engage with the world confidently.

Developing body awareness is a crucial step toward self-care and personal empowerment. By tuning into the internal landscape of bodily sensations, individuals can better understand their needs and respond with appropriate actions. This self-attunement nurtures a sense of agency and encourages exploration into the self, facilitating personal discovery. As individuals become more adept at listening to and interpreting body signals, they can embark on a transformative journey of self-awareness that culminates in empowerment and growth.

Incorporating body awareness into daily life is not merely about honing physical skills but about achieving a deeper unity with the self. This awareness serves as a foundation for a richer understanding of personal experience, where the subtle language of the body becomes a tool for navigating the complexities of life. As body awareness is integrated into one's routine, it becomes a guide and companion, offering insights and nurturing a more profound connection to life's myriad dimensions. Through consistent practice, the power of body awareness unfolds, revealing its potential to transform how individuals relate to themselves and the world. The journey to connect more intimately with one's body opens doors to greater emotional intelligence, resilience, and empowerment. As individuals embrace this path, they awaken an inner force characterized by harmony, balance, and mindfulness, thus propelling them toward an existence imbued with awareness and intention. This path not only fosters personal empowerment but enriches the broader journey of self-discovery, inviting each individual to explore the depth and breadth of their potential.

Healing Through Movement

Healing through movement offers a holistic approach to well-being, harnessing the body's natural ability to heal and transform. Movement is more than just physical exercise; it is a vital expression of life that encompasses emotional, psychological, and spiritual dimensions. The therapeutic potential of movement is grounded in its ability to facilitate emotional release, enhance mental clarity, and promote physical health.

Extensive evidence supports the efficacy of movement therapies in improving mental health conditions such as depression and anxiety. Research has demonstrated that engaging in physical activity can be as effective as medication in alleviating symptoms of these disorders. Movement stimulates the production of endorphins, neurotransmitters that generate feelings of happiness and well-being. By releasing these chemicals, the body naturally combats negative emotions, offering a non-invasive and empowering alternative to traditional treatments.

Movement therapies are particularly instrumental in addressing trauma and are recognized for their cultural sensitivity and liberation-informed approach. These therapies are tailored to respect the diverse backgrounds and experiences of participants, creating a welcoming environment that acknowledges and honors individuality. This sensitivity ensures that movement practices are inclusive and accessible to all, reinforcing the healing journey by acknowledging each participant's unique path and story.

The communal aspect of movement enhances the healing process by providing essential social support. Participation in group activities such as team sports, yoga classes, or community walks fosters a sense of belonging and connection. This communal setting not only motivates individuals but also offers emotional support, which is crucial for recovery and personal growth. The shared experience of movement creates bonds that transcend individual differences, promoting an inclusive atmosphere of mutual encouragement and shared joy.

Incorporating professional guidance in movement practices is integral, especially for those navigating trauma. Trauma-informed instructors create safe environments where participants can explore physical activities without fear of judgment or pressure. These professionals understand the nuances of trauma and provide personalized movement plans that respect individual boundaries. By facilitating secure and progressive exploration, these instructors help cultivate positive attitudes toward movement, encouraging individuals to rediscover their bodies in empowered and joyful ways.

Inclusivity in movement therapy workshops is fundamental, emphasizing acceptance of all bodies and experience levels. These workshops promote self-expression and empowerment, helping participants shed self-doubt and transcend limiting beliefs. When environments are inclusive and supportive, participants feel free to explore movement without constraints, leading to profound breakthroughs in both body awareness and self-confidence. It fosters a sense of liberation that is integral to healing and self-discovery.

Diverse modalities offer varied pathways for healing through movement, each bringing unique benefits to the body, mind, and soul. Dance therapy, yoga, and Qi Gong are among the many forms utilized to facilitate this integration. These practices reduce anxiety, encourage relaxation, and align energy, contributing to holistic well-being. Dance therapy, for instance, utilizes rhythm and expression to unlock emotional truths, while yoga combines breath and postures to instill peace and balance. Qi Gong harmonizes energy flow, nurturing both the physical and spiritual self.

Practical applications of movement healing can be found in workshops and classes that offer tools for releasing stress and cultivating joy. By integrating different movement modalities, these sessions provide opportunities for body awareness and personal development. Participants learn to release tension, embrace their physicality, and connect with others, cultivating a sense of belonging and community. These elements are critical for healing and transformation, fostering environments where individuals can thrive and explore new dimensions of themselves.

Movement is a universal language that transcends cultural and personal barriers, connecting individuals to their innate strength and resilience. It offers a dynamic process of healing that is as diverse and individual as those who engage in it. By embracing the power of movement, individuals unlock a transformative pathway to self-awareness, empowerment, and holistic well-being.

Inclusion of movement in daily life is not only a tool for managing physical health but also a potent strategy for emotional and psychological resilience. Sustainable healing through movement involves a commitment to listen to the body's cues, trust its wisdom, and engage with it in respectful dialogue. Movement becomes a reflection of one's inner state and a channel for cultivating presence and mindfulness.

Engaging with movement as a healing practice invites individuals to participate actively in their health journey. It empowers them to reclaim agency over their bodies and emotions, facilitating a reconnection with their sense of vitality. This reconnection serves as a catalyst for self-discovery, offering insights and revelations that inform and guide the broader journey of life. As participants embrace movement's healing power, they awaken a profound inner force that supports and sustains them.

The transformative nature of movement empowers individuals to discover strength in vulnerability, freedom in expression, and peace in alignment. It calls upon them to explore the vast potential of their bodies in concert with their minds, emerging with a renewed sense of wholeness and unity.

Recognizing the profound impact of movement on personal empowerment and self-discovery is vital. As individuals integrate these practices into their lives, they experience a blossoming of both body and spirit, paving the way for enriched existence. Through movement, a harmonious balance between body, mind, and soul is achieved, guiding individuals toward a fulfilling and empowered life filled with discovery and growth.

Integrating Mind and Body

Integrating the mind and body is a profound journey toward a holistic understanding of oneself, a synergy that unlocks new dimensions of personal empowerment and self-discovery. The mind and body are no longer seen as disparate entities but as parts of a unified whole that influence and reflect each other in complex ways. This integration is not merely a metaphorical concept but a practical reality that can be cultivated through specific techniques, offering deep transformations in emotional, psychological, and physical well-being.

Mind-body integration techniques are at the forefront of helping individuals connect with their inherent capacity for self-healing and growth. Practices such as mindfulness and guided visualization play a pivotal role in enhancing this connection. Mindfulness involves cultivating an awareness of the present moment, allowing individuals to observe their thoughts and bodily sensations non-judgmentally. Guided visualization complements this by engaging the imagination to explore scenarios that encourage relaxation and positive mental states. Together, these practices foster confidence, intrinsic motivation, and self-efficacy—empowering individuals to align their actions with their authentic values and desires.

A whole-person integrative approach, embodied by frameworks like the Wheel of Health, emphasizes the interconnectedness of various life domains. This model encourages looking beyond symptoms to explore the broader context of an individual's life, incorporating elements such as lifestyle behaviors, emotional factors, and social connections. Through this lens, health and wellness are seen as dynamic and holistic processes, facilitating a more comprehensive understanding of one's needs and potentials.

Embodiment therapy integrates physical sensations and movements into the therapeutic process, recognizing the profound influence of the body on emotional and psychological states. Somatic therapy, yoga therapy, and movement therapy use bodily sensations and movements to facilitate healing and transformation. This approach highlights the significance of listening to the body's messages and using them as guides for therapy. By connecting deeply with physical sensations, individuals can process and release stored tensions, work through traumatic experiences, and discover new pathways to emotional resilience and strength.

Embodiment practices offer numerous benefits, including stress regulation, enhanced emotional well-being, and improved overall health. Mindful movement and dance movement therapy are particularly effective in releasing tensions and fostering a joyful connection with one's body. By engaging in these practices, individuals can explore bodily awareness, which aids in processing emotions and finding balance in a seemingly chaotic world. These practices not only promote psychological healing but also encourage a playful and authentic engagement with life.

The integration of mind-body processes is enriched by applying adult learning principles, which focus on self-directed learning and hands-on involvement. This approach ensures that the learning is relevant and practical, with a direct impact on the participant's life. By framing learning through these principles, individuals engage more fully with embodiment practices, ensuring the incorporation of these insights into their daily experiences.

Practical applications of embodiment practices are diverse and adaptable, catering to the varied needs and preferences of individuals. Options include online classes and private therapy sessions, designed to offer structured and supportive environments where individuals can explore their physical and emotional health. Weekly online embodiment classes and guided movement therapies provide an accessible platform for individuals to connect with their bodies and emotions, enhancing personal growth in a safe environment.

Key tools and frameworks, like the VHC Funnel and the IVA funnel, have been developed to integrate motivational interviewing and mind-body processes into coaching practices. These tools streamline the coaching process, ensuring that individuals receive effective and personalized support. By adopting these tools, coaches and therapists can better facilitate the journey of self-discovery and empowerment, guiding individuals toward their true potential.

The process of integrating mind and body is transformative. It invites individuals to explore the profound intelligence of the body, often revealing insights and patterns that the cognitive mind alone cannot uncover. By embracing both mental and physical experiences as vital sources of wisdom, individuals develop a more nuanced understanding of themselves and their interactions with the world.

Engaging in practices that marry mental focus with physical movement produces a synchrony that enriches life. This integration catalyzes change by unveiling hidden aspects of self and dissolving barriers to personal growth. The impact of such embodied consciousness extends beyond individual benefit, enhancing relationships and fostering a community of understanding and empathy.

Through continual practice and awareness, the integration of mind and body becomes not a mere exercise, but a way of life—an enduring commitment to living authentically and fully. This journey revitalizes the connection with oneself and the world, promoting an existence characterized by intentionality, presence, and joy. As individuals cultivate this deeper connection, they awaken to the richness of their potential and the boundless opportunities for growth and transformation that life offers. The integrated mind-body experience truly empowers individuals to embrace their lives with renewed vigor and an enlightened perspective, laying the foundation for transformative personal empowerment and holistic well-being.

CHAPTER 5: Empowering Beliefs for Growth

Identifying Limiting Beliefs

Identifying limiting beliefs is a vital step in the journey of personal empowerment and self-discovery. These beliefs act as invisible barriers, hindering personal growth and potential. Often perceived as indisputable truths, they manifest in the form of negative self-perceptions, unfounded fears, or misconceptions that restrict individuals from exploring new horizons and achieving their goals. The power of limiting beliefs lies in their subtlety and persistence, making it crucial to uncover and address them to foster a more authentic and fulfilling life.

The origins of limiting beliefs are varied and deeply rooted in one's upbringing and experiences. Family values play a significant role; beliefs and perceptions held by parents, grandparents, or other influential family members often become an integral part of an individual's mindset from a young age. These beliefs, whether verbally expressed or implied through behaviors and attitudes, can shape perceptions about oneself and the world.

Significant life experiences also contribute to the formation of limiting beliefs. Negative experiences, such as failures or criticism, can leave lasting impressions, causing individuals to adopt beliefs that protect them from perceived future harm. For example, a child who frequently hears they struggle with math problems might carry the belief "I'm not good at math" into adulthood, influencing career choices and educational opportunities.

Educational environments and influential figures like teachers and mentors also mold limiting beliefs. A comment from a teacher, no matter how unintended, can reinforce self-doubt or fear of inadequacy. The authority that educators hold can make their opinions seem absolute, imbuing their judgments or perceptions with undue significance.

To empower personal growth, it is essential to identify these limiting beliefs. This process begins with paying attention to patterns of negative self-talk and fear-based thinking. Statements like "I can't do this" or "I'm not capable" are classic indicators of underlying limiting beliefs that need examination. Recognizing these patterns allows individuals to bring subconscious beliefs into the conscious mind, making them amenable to change.

Awareness is the first step in overcoming limiting beliefs. Self-reflection is vital, allowing individuals to explore the roots of these beliefs and understand how they have shaped their behaviors and decisions. Feedback from trusted friends, family, or mentors can provide valuable perspectives that help illuminate blind spots. Once identified, challenging the validity of these beliefs becomes crucial. This involves questioning their truth and seeking out evidence that contradicts them. For instance, instead of accepting "I'm not good at public speaking," one might recall instances where communication was effective, thereby reframing the belief into "I am capable of improving my public speaking skills."

Various therapeutic interventions can support this process, notably cognitive-behavioral therapy (CBT), which focuses on identifying and restructuring negative thinking patterns. CBT provides tools to confront limiting beliefs systematically and replace them with constructive alternatives. By working with professionals trained in these techniques, individuals can gain insights into their thought processes and develop more empowering beliefs.

Practical strategies also play a significant role in this journey. Setting realistic goals helps create evidence of competence and achievement, progressively dismantling limiting beliefs. Engaging in mindfulness practices cultivates self-awareness and detachment from negative thought patterns, empowering individuals to observe their thoughts without judgment. Participating in activities that directly challenge limiting beliefs, such as joining a debate club to overcome a fear of public speaking, reinforces resilience and demonstrates personal capacity for growth.

In workplace settings, it is beneficial to connect personal work to larger organizational goals, fostering a sense of purpose and alignment that counters limiting beliefs. Encouraging a supportive team culture where achievements are recognized and individual contributions valued also helps lay the groundwork for a positive and empowering belief system.

Empowering beliefs are essential for personal growth, aiding resilience and nurturing success. These beliefs encourage individuals to view challenges as opportunities for learning and growth, adopting a growth mindset that emphasizes effort and perseverance over fixed limitations. Positive self-talk replaces doubt and negativity with affirmations of capability and potential. Additionally, fostering an environment that supports and values personal development creates fertile ground for these new, empowering beliefs to flourish.

Replacing limiting beliefs with empowering ones transforms an individual's self-confidence and motivation, leading to enhanced well-being. This transformation fosters a belief system that is adaptive and growth-oriented, encouraging continued personal development and the pursuit of excellence.

Incorporating the practice of identifying and addressing limiting beliefs opens new pathways for self-discovery and empowerment. The process is one of gradual unveiling and transformation, allowing individuals to shed outdated or harmful perceptions that no longer serve them. In their place, a renewed self-awareness and belief in one's potential take root, guiding them towards their authentic selves.

By actively reshaping beliefs, individuals liberate themselves from the confines of self-imposed barriers, awakening to possibilities that were previously obscured. This journey of transformation not only empowers individuals but also invigorates their engagement with life, inspiring them to seize opportunities with confidence and clarity.

Ultimately, the exploration and transformation of limiting beliefs is a continuous process, woven into the fabric of personal growth and discovery. As individuals navigate through this landscape, they embark on a journey of authenticity and empowerment, lighting the way with newfound insight and understanding. The path to personal empowerment is illuminated by the courage to challenge limitations and the conviction to cultivate empowering beliefs that fuel growth and self-realization.

Strategies to Overcome Obstacles

Overcoming obstacles is a crucial aspect of personal growth, requiring both strategic approaches and empowering beliefs. As individuals navigate life's challenges, adopting effective strategies can transform potential setbacks into opportunities for advancement. Each obstacle presents a unique opportunity to cultivate resilience, expand understanding, and reinforce a commitment to personal development.

Adopting a growth mindset is fundamental in this transformative journey. This mindset, introduced by psychologist Carol Dweck, encompasses viewing challenges not as insurmountable barriers but as opportunities for learning and growth. It encourages individuals to embrace failure as a natural part of the learning process, promoting perseverance and self-reflection. By adopting this perspective, individuals become more resilient, developing new skills and insights that fuel continuous personal expansion.

Maintaining a positive mindset and an optimistic outlook is essential for navigating difficulties with determination. Believing in oneself and cultivating positivity can significantly influence how challenges are perceived and handled. Optimism fosters a sense of possibility, empowering individuals to approach obstacles with confidence and a proactive attitude. This positive approach not only aids in managing stress but also enhances creativity and problem-solving abilities, enabling individuals to find innovative solutions to complex challenges.

Effective goal-setting and accountability are also crucial in overcoming obstacles. Setting clear and achievable goals provides direction and focus, breaking down daunting tasks into manageable steps. This strategy involves tracking progress and celebrating milestones to maintain motivation and momentum. By acknowledging small victories, individuals build confidence and remain engaged with their objectives. This structured approach ensures that goals are not only attainable but also continuously evaluated and adjusted according to ongoing experiences and learning.

Stepping out of one's comfort zone is an integral component of personal growth. Comfort zones create a safety net that often limits potential and exploration. Growth occurs when individuals challenge themselves to reach beyond familiar boundaries. Starting with small steps and gradually increasing the level of challenge helps build confidence and capability. Embracing fear and uncertainty as part of the growth process allows individuals to learn from failures, viewing them as valuable lessons rather than insurmountable setbacks. The importance of seeking support and guidance cannot be overstated.

Surrounding oneself with a supportive network of loved ones, mentors, and peers provides the encouragement and motivation needed to overcome obstacles. This network serves as a resource for advice, perspective, and feedback, helping individuals to navigate challenges with greater insight and courage. The presence of supportive relationships fosters a sense of belonging and understanding, enhancing emotional resilience and personal strength.

Self-care and self-reflection are vital practices for sustaining energy and motivation. Prioritizing self-care ensures that physical, emotional, and mental well-being is maintained, allowing individuals to function optimally despite challenges. Practices such as mindfulness, exercise, and adequate rest are essential to preserving vitality. Self-reflection fosters self-awareness, helping individuals to identify internal barriers and challenge negative thought patterns. By embracing a growth mindset, individuals welcome change and learning, cultivating a flexible and adaptive approach to life's challenges.

Embracing change and learning from failure is a hallmark of resilient individuals. Viewing failures as learning opportunities helps to cultivate a culture of continuous growth and improvement.

Analyzing what went wrong, extracting valuable lessons, and applying those insights to future efforts are strategies that enhance adaptability and success. This approach not only mitigates the fear of failure but also inspires a proactive attitude toward overcoming obstacles.

Integration of these strategies into daily practice empowers individuals to navigate challenges with confidence and ingenuity. By consistently applying empowering beliefs and practices, individuals strengthen their inner resources, enabling them to transform obstacles into stepping stones for growth. This empowerment fuels a journey of self-discovery and advancement, contributing to a life characterized by purpose, fulfillment, and resilience.

Through commitment to lifelong learning and the cultivation of a mindset that celebrates growth and adaptability, individuals are well-equipped to face the complexities of an ever-changing world. As they embrace the inherent challenges and opportunities of life, they become architects of their own development, shaping a future that aligns with their vision and aspirations. By embodying these empowering strategies, individuals unlock the potential within themselves, discovering the limitless possibilities that personal growth affords.

The synergy created by these approaches fosters an environment where obstacles are transformed into opportunities. This environment nurtures a culture of resilience, enabling individuals to persist in the face of adversity and confidently pursue their goals. Through dedication and intentionality, individuals harness the power within, guiding them toward meaningful experiences and the realization of their fullest potential.

Building a Growth Mindset

In an era characterized by rapid technological and geopolitical shifts, cultivating a growth mindset emerges as a pivotal strategy for navigating an increasingly complex world. A growth mindset—coined by psychologist Carol Dweck—endorses the belief that abilities and intelligence can be developed through dedication, effort, and learning. This stands in stark contrast to a fixed mindset, which holds that these qualities are immutable and static. Developing a growth mindset not only empowers individuals to face uncertainties with confidence but also fosters a lifelong passion for learning and self-improvement.

In *2025*, the World Economic Forum underscored the critical need for an adaptive mindset to keep pace with the rapid developments reshaping our global landscape. The ability to adapt to new technologies, shifts in marketplaces, and evolving governmental regulations is paramount. This necessitates a mindset that embraces change and seeks opportunity within challenges. By adopting a growth mindset, individuals become better equipped to learn from experiences and cultivate adaptability—skills essential for thriving in today's dynamic environment.

Achieving a growth mindset involves adopting techniques to transition from fixed perceptions to a more adaptive and fluid approach. An effective starting point is conducting an inventory of one's current mindset, identifying moments of fixed thinking that may hinder development. This involves recognizing areas where growth may be stymied by internalized notions of limitation. By acknowledging these areas, individuals can start to shift their focus from static evaluations to dynamic growth potentials.

Focusing on the process and strategy rather than the end result is another key technique. This perspective emphasizes learning and personal growth over immediate success or failure, viewing setbacks as valuable opportunities for improvement. Embracing challenges as part of a learning journey encourages resilience and reduces the fear associated with failure. It transforms failures into stepping stones for growth, nurturing an environment where innovation and creativity flourish.

Resilience and grit are integral components of a growth mindset. As highlighted by psychologist Angela Duckworth, grit refers to perseverance and passion for long-term goals. This quality drives individuals to remain steadfast in their pursuits, even in the face of adversity. A growth mindset enhances resilience by shifting focus toward what can be learned from a challenge rather than the disappointment it presents. Over time, this leads to enhanced performance and a robust capacity to overcome obstacles.

The application of a growth mindset extends beyond personal development, permeating professional and legislative contexts as well. In professional settings, a growth mindset fosters resilience, creativity, and an enthusiasm for learning—all crucial for success in diverse fields. Teams that embody a growth mindset approach challenges with innovation, viewing them as chances to refine skills and expand knowledge. It cultivates a culture of collaboration and continuous improvement, essential attributes in a rapidly evolving workforce.

For the year *2025*, practical steps to embed a growth mindset into daily life and work include engaging with new technologies such as artificial intelligence, enhancing skill sets like questionnaire design, and adopting proactive approaches to effecting change. Embracing the mantra of being the change you wish to see encourages individuals to actively incorporate growth-oriented behaviors into their routines. This proactive stance creates alignment between personal values and actions, guiding individuals toward meaningful and impactful growth.

Balancing growth with well-being is crucial to sustaining a growth mindset. While the pursuit of development and achievement is vital, real success lies in setting boundaries and ensuring time for rest and reflection. This balance guards against the traps of hustle culture, which can lead to burnout and counterproductive stress. Instead, integrating downtime and self-care into routines promotes sustainable growth and maintains well-being, ensuring that personal development does not come at the cost of health.

The journey toward building a growth mindset is one of transformation and empowerment. By embracing strategies that promote learning and adaptability, individuals cultivate a mindset that encourages relentless curiosity and the courage to explore new possibilities. This mindset becomes a lens through which life's complexities are viewed, revealing potential within challenges and highlighting paths to continual improvement.

Fostering a growth mindset nurtures an inner force that motivates individuals to seek purpose and relish the process of development. It forms the foundation upon which empowering beliefs are built, driving the pursuit of aspirations and sustaining enthusiasm for life-long learning. Engaging with a growth mindset invites individuals to expand their horizons, unlocking reservoirs of potential and fostering a more fulfilling and resilient approach to life.

Through the lens of a growth mindset, challenges transform into chapters of an evolving narrative—stories of perseverance, learning, and achievement. By committing to this mindset, individuals not only empower themselves but contribute to a broader culture that values adaptability, innovation, and collective progress. This dynamic approach to personal and professional growth equips individuals to navigate the unpredictable currents of modern life, embracing change with optimism and a steadfast belief in their capacity to grow.

CHAPTER 6: Navigating Emotional Landscapes

Understanding Your Emotions

Understanding emotions is a fundamental aspect of personal development and empowerment, enabling individuals to navigate the complexities of life with poise and insight. Central to this understanding is the concept of emotional intelligence (EQ), which encompasses the ability to recognize, comprehend, and manage one's own emotions while also being attuned to the emotional states of others. Unlike IQ, which assesses cognitive prowess, EQ provides the tools necessary for effective interaction in personal and professional settings, significantly impacting overall success and satisfaction.

Emotional intelligence involves several core competencies. The ability to recognize and accurately identify emotions in oneself and others lays the foundation for understanding how emotions influence thoughts and behaviors. This awareness enables individuals to perceive emotional cues and respond appropriately, fostering more effective communication and stronger relationships. Understanding emotions also involves leveraging emotional information to guide decision-making and behavior, incorporating emotional nuances into the cognitive processes that drive choices and actions.

Managing and regulating emotions is another critical component of emotional intelligence. This skill allows individuals to adapt to varying environments, maintaining emotional balance amidst challenges. The capacity to control emotional responses, especially during high-stress situations, promotes resilience and stability. Responding appropriately to the emotions of others further refines interpersonal interactions, creating a foundation of empathy and mutual respect that is crucial for successful collaboration and conflict resolution.

The development of emotional intelligence offers profound benefits, distinguishing itself as a dynamic attribute that can be cultivated throughout life. Unlike IQ, which tends to remain stable, EQ can be enhanced with purposeful practice and awareness. Research consistently demonstrates a strong correlation between high EQ and professional achievement, highlighting its role in effective leadership and team dynamics. Leaders with robust emotional intelligence inspire and retain employees, fostering environments conducive to growth and innovation.

In recent years, organizations have increasingly prioritized emotional intelligence as a key factor in achieving corporate objectives. In *2025*, the focus on collaboration, customer satisfaction, and employee engagement underscores the significance of EQ in navigating organizational goals. Emotional intelligence directly impacts these areas by facilitating open communication, enhancing problem-solving capabilities, and promoting an inclusive workplace culture. As a result, cultivating EQ within professional settings has become a strategic priority.

The intersection of artificial intelligence and emotional intelligence represents an intriguing advancement. With the development of sophisticated AI models, such as ChatGPT-4, technology is beginning to match or even exceed human performance in emotional intelligence assessments. This development presents opportunities to leverage AI in educational and professional training contexts. AI systems, when supervised by skilled professionals, can aid in coaching and conflict management, offering new modalities for enhancing emotional intelligence in diverse settings.

The practical applications of emotional intelligence in personal empowerment are extensive. Understanding and developing EQ contributes to building robust and meaningful relationships by nurturing empathy and effective communication. High EQ enables better decision-making by integrating emotional considerations into the cognitive processes that underpin judgments. This holistic approach to decision-making results in choices that are not only rational but also emotionally intelligent, balancing facts with feelings for more balanced outcomes.

Managing stress is another advantage of honed emotional intelligence. By cultivating self-awareness and emotional regulation, individuals can navigate stressful environments with greater ease, reducing anxiety and enhancing adaptability. This adaptability is particularly valuable in today's fast-paced world, where changing conditions demand flexibility and innovation. In addition, motivating oneself and others becomes more attainable with improved emotional intelligence, as understanding emotional drivers helps to inspire action and sustain momentum in pursuing personal and collective goals.

The path to enhancing emotional intelligence and understanding one's emotions involves both reflective and active elements. Regular self-inquiry, mindfulness practices, and feedback from trusted relationships foster greater emotional awareness and insight. Embracing new challenges that involve emotional dynamics, such as public speaking or leading a team, further develops EQ by providing real-world contexts in which to practice empathy, regulation, and adaptation.

Integrating emotional intelligence into everyday life enriches the journey of personal growth and discovery. It empowers individuals to approach life's emotional landscapes with sensitivity and understanding, transforming emotional challenges into opportunities for deeper connection and learning. By committing to this exploration, individuals not only enhance their connections with others but also with themselves, leading to a more harmonious and fulfilling existence.

Through the cultivation of emotional intelligence, individuals experience a profound shift towards greater clarity, resilience, and empathy. This journey shapes their approach to both expected and unforeseen challenges, embedding a sense of ease and confidence that bolsters personal and professional aspirations. In navigating the winding paths of emotional landscapes, individuals unlock a vital force within themselves that guides them towards a balanced and enriched life, harmonizing rationality with emotional wisdom.

Emotional Freedom Techniques

Emotional Freedom Techniques (EFT), commonly known as "tapping," represent a powerful modality for addressing emotional distress and enhancing overall well-being. This method, distinct in its approach yet rooted in principles similar to acupuncture, involves tapping on specific points of the body. These points align with energy meridians, and tapping them stimulates a release of energy blockages, facilitating emotional and physical healing without the need for needles. EFT serves as a pathway to foster personal empowerment by allowing individuals to take an active role in their emotional regulation and healing processes.

EFT's effectiveness has garnered increasing recognition within the therapeutic community, with a growing body of research supporting its use as an evidence-based technique. Prominent figures such as trauma expert Bessel van der Kolk have endorsed its potential in treating anxiety, depression, post-traumatic stress disorder (PTSD), and chronic pain. The mechanism by which EFT operates involves the reduction of cortisol levels, a hormone often elevated in response to stress. By modulating stress responses, EFT provides users with a practical tool to manage emotional disturbances, contributing to improved mental health and overall vitality.

The practical applications of EFT are extensive, making it feasible to integrate into daily routines regardless of one's schedule. Its simplicity allows for practice in a variety of settings, whether as a brief interruption to a busy workday or as a dedicated home practice. EFT empowers users with self-regulation techniques, enabling them to independently address and alleviate emotional distress as it arises. The ease of learning and implementing EFT makes it a valuable tool for both individual and professional use.

Educational initiatives and training programs have proliferated, promoting the acquisition of EFT skills among clinicians and the general public. Programs such as the "EFT Tapping for Clinicians" course and the "Tapping World Summit 2025" provide comprehensive training, from introductory skills to advanced techniques, alongside continuing education credits for professionals. These educational efforts underscore the growing acceptance and integration of EFT into mainstream therapeutic practices, establishing a foundation for its sustained application across diverse contexts.

The benefits of EFT extend beyond emotional regulation; they encompass significant improvements in physical conditions as well. By neutralizing emotional distress, EFT can ameliorate physiological symptoms often associated with stress and anxiety, such as headaches, muscle tension, and chronic pain. Its role in enhancing performance and reinforcing overall health makes EFT a multifaceted tool for personal development and well-being.

Community initiatives further demonstrate the versatility of EFT, highlighting its applicability in various professional arenas. Programs like the "Creating Calm with Emotional Freedom Techniques" series aim to mitigate stress among professionals, including attorneys, showing how

EFT can be tailored to support individuals working in high-stress careers. Through these initiatives, EFT's capacity to cultivate calm, resilience, and well-being is shared and celebrated.

To understand EFT, one must begin with its foundational techniques, which involve identifying the specific emotional or physical issue to be addressed. This focus sets the intention for the tapping session. Practitioners then tap on a series of meridian points on the body, often beginning with the karate chop point on the side of the hand, while voicing phrases that acknowledge the issue and affirm acceptance. This combination of physically engaging with the body and cognitively affirming one's current state fosters a holistic release of blocked energy. As the tapping sequence progresses, individuals are encouraged to shift from acknowledging distress to reinforcing empowering beliefs.

If you search online, you'll find that testimonials and case studies highlight the profound impact of EFT on individuals managing diverse emotional challenges. Users report significant relief from symptoms of anxiety and depression, often experiencing a renewed sense of clarity and calm. These personal accounts not only validate the effectiveness of EFT but also inspire new users to explore this modality as a viable tool in their emotional toolkit.

EFT can be seamlessly integrated with other self-discovery and empowerment practices, enhancing the journey toward personal growth. It complements mindfulness, meditation, and cognitive reframing techniques by providing a tangible method to address and release emotional blockages. In this synergy, EFT reinforces the principles of self-awareness and empowerment, promoting a deeper connection to one's emotional landscape.

The empowerment gained through EFT lies in its ability to facilitate self-regulation. By understanding and mastering this technique, individuals can autonomously manage their emotional states and physical well-being. This empowerment is transformative, as it encourages a proactive approach to health and wellness, supporting a sustainable path to personal development.

Incorporating EFT into one's life offers a versatile and effective means of navigating emotional landscapes. By aligning mental and physical processes, EFT nurtures a comprehensive understanding of well-being, fostering inner strength and self-discovery. Whether used as a standalone practice or integrated into broader therapeutic frameworks, EFT provides a valuable asset in the pursuit of emotional balance and resilience.

The practice of EFT signifies more than a technique; it represents a commitment to self-care and healing. By embracing this practice, individuals gain access to a method that enhances emotional intelligence, fosters resilience, and cultivates a harmonious relationship with themselves. Through EFT, the journey towards personal empowerment becomes a reality, encouraging each individual to embrace their capacity for change and transformation.

Embracing Vulnerability and Strength

Embracing vulnerability as a form of strength revolutionizes how individuals perceive the intersections of fragility and resilience within themselves. At its core, vulnerability signifies the openness to acknowledge and express genuine emotions, even when it breeds discomfort or uncertainty. This process embodies courage, demanding the fortitude to step into emotional exposure and authenticity. By embracing vulnerability, individuals not only challenge societal norms that associate vulnerability with weakness but also redefine it as a profound source of empowerment.

The journey toward embracing vulnerability begins with the acceptance of imperfections and the willingness to confront emotions head-on. This acceptance is a catalyst for personal growth, as it fosters self-awareness and emotional intelligence. These attributes are indispensable in understanding and managing emotions effectively. In recognizing one's susceptibilities, individuals gain insights into their emotional processes, enabling them to navigate their inner landscapes with clarity and intention. This awareness urges individuals to move beyond perfunctory self-perceptions and invest in deeper explorations of the self.

Engaging with vulnerability cultivates an inner resilience that fortifies individuals against the vagaries of life's challenges. Resilience emerges not from denying fears or discomforts but from addressing them with quiet courage. This courage is not always grandiose but often takes the form of silent determination to confront what lies beneath the surface. Such encounters reinforce trust in oneself, affirming the capacity to survive and thrive despite adversities. By meeting vulnerability with courage, individuals amass the strength needed to endure difficulties and emerge fortified.

Authenticity forms the backbone of embracing vulnerability, conferring both clarity and empowerment. By clarifying personal identity and boundaries, individuals equip themselves with the tools to engage with life honestly and compassionately. Authenticity setting confident boundaries, facilitates ensuring interactions are genuine and respectful of personal values. This alignment of actions and beliefs fosters meaningful relationships, where emotional connection and mutual understanding deepen.

Living fully and necessitates mutual embracing vulnerability, which often involves stepping into spaces where judgment or rejection loom. Vulnerability invites risk, fostering environments where growth and learning take precedence over perfection or infallibility. By viewing failures as lessons rather than deterrents, individuals create room for evolution and adaptability. Engaging in tough conversations and confronting fears opened channels for personal development and empathy, fortifying emotional intelligence and resilience.

Integrating vulnerability into daily practices begins with incremental steps. It involves acknowledging and actively engaging with emotions instead of suppressing them. Practicing vulnerability might include sharing feelings openly with trusted individuals or reflecting on emotional experiences in a journal. Programs like the series at the Tampa Bay Center of Relational Psychology provide structured approaches, aiding individuals in navigating vulnerability constructively and consciously.

Facing negative emotions and articulating truths restores personal peace and self-esteem. Embracing this often uncomfortable process results in emotional liberation, relieving burdens that hinder personal growth. Confronting emotional challenges, rather than allowing them to fester, empowers individuals to reclaim their narrative and forge pathways toward healing and fulfillment.

By embracing vulnerability, individuals embark on a transformative journey of self-discovery and empowerment. This journey cultivates a deepened understanding of personal emotions and a richer engagement with the world. Vulnerability invites an authentic experience of life, where strength arises from the ability to be open, truthful, and compassionate. The fusion of vulnerability and strength not only nurtures personal resilience but also inspires others, creating ripples of empowerment and understanding across wider communities.

The decision to embrace vulnerability encompasses the acceptance of imperfections and a commitment to authenticity. This choice cultivates an environment where individuals can thrive emotionally and relationally, fostering a spectrum of experiences that enrich life. Understanding that vulnerability is a journey rather than a destination allows for continual growth, where each step reinforces strength and courage.

The practice of embracing vulnerability as strength reveals the profound capacity of individuals to connect with their inner forces and navigate emotional landscapes with grace. This alignment with vulnerability and resilience amplifies personal empowerment and fuels a vibrant, connected, and deeply fulfilling life journey. It reshapes the narrative around vulnerability, celebrating it as an integral component of human strength and potential.

CHAPTER 7: Cultivating Inner Resilience

Building Resilience through Challenges

Building resilience in the face of challenges is akin to strengthening the fibers of a complex, yet remarkably adaptable fabric. This fabric is woven with threads of connection, wellness, healthy thinking, and meaning—each contributing to personal fortitude and the capacity to recover from adversity. The journey to resilience is not a solitary path; it embraces relationships, health, and purpose as cornerstones.

Connection serves as one of the fundamental pillars of resilience. Humans are inherently social beings, and strong relationships provide emotional support and practical assistance. These networks act as buffers against stress, offering perspective and encouragement during trying times. Whether through friends, family, or community groups, forming and maintaining meaningful connections ensures that individuals are not alone, and provides a safety net of support and inspiration. Relying on and contributing to these networks fosters resilience, enriching both individual lives and community ties.

Wellness encompasses the physical and mental health practices that form the foundation of resilience. Engaging in regular physical activity, maintaining a balanced diet, and ensuring adequate sleep are critical to physical well-being. These habits support mental health, boosting mood, energy, and cognitive function--all integral to managing stress. In tandem, mental health practices such as mindfulness and self-care nourish the mind, promoting a peaceful and balanced inner landscape. Together, wellness practices create a state of readiness, equipping individuals to face life's fluctuations with buoyancy and strength.

Healthy thinking is a transformative component of resilience, characterized by positive and adaptive thought patterns. Techniques from cognitive behavioral therapy (CBT) are particularly effective in cultivating this aspect of resilience. CBT involves identifying and reshaping negative or dysfunctional thoughts, replacing them with more constructive and affirming beliefs. This cognitive restructuring enhances coping strategies and fosters a mindset oriented toward solutions and growth.

By shifting perspectives and challenging negative narratives, individuals develop a more resilient outlook, prepared to engage with challenges as opportunities for learning and adaptation.

Finding meaning in life acts as a compass, providing motivation and direction. A sense of purpose animates resilience, offering a larger vision that guides decisions and actions during challenging times. Cultivating meaning can derive from contributing to causes beyond oneself, pursuing passions, or aligning daily actions with core values. When adversity strikes, these sources of meaning offer solace and inspiration, reaffirming one's place and purpose in a complex and sometimes chaotic world.

Therapy techniques such as CBT enhance resilience by addressing and modifying thought patterns and behaviors that undermine coping mechanisms. Mindfulness practices offer exhaustive tools for building emotional resilience. Through present-moment awareness and acceptance, mindfulness encourages a non-judgmental attitude towards thoughts and feelings, enhancing the ability to manage stress and navigate emotional turbulence.

This practice fosters an openness to experience, where individuals can engage with their emotions fully, yet maintain a grounded sense of self.

Embracing exposure and acceptance further reinforces resilience. Exposure therapy involves confronting fears and anxieties in a controlled, gradual manner, reducing the power of fear and enhancing confidence. By challenging negative associations, this therapy empowers individuals to face uncertainties with bravery and assurance. Complementary to this is the practice of acceptance, which facilitates observing thoughts and feelings without judgment. Acceptance nurtures emotional fluidity, allowing individuals to acknowledge and release difficult emotions, rather than becoming entangled in their grip.

Focusing on controllable aspects of a situation is a strategic practice in fostering resilience. This shift in perspective empowers individuals, affirming their ability to influence outcomes and navigate challenges effectively. By emphasizing aspects within one's control, individuals can allocate energy and resources more efficiently, fostering a sense of agency and efficacy.

Positive reframing transforms challenges into opportunities for growth. Viewing obstacles not as barriers but as catalysts for development can fundamentally alter one's response to adversity. This reframing encourages a positive outlook and fosters resilience by valuing the lessons embedded within each experience. Embracing failure as an opportunity for growth nurtures a mindset resilient to setbacks and open to innovation.

Facing fears directly is a robust exercise in resilience-building. As individuals confront and gradually overcome fears, whether through exposure therapy or incremental challenges, they enhance their capacity to handle adversity. This practice cultivates courage and reinforces the belief in one's capability to surmount obstacles. Growth occurs in the space where fear is confronted and transformed into a pathway to strength.

Social support networks are vital to emotional resilience. Engaging with friends, family, mentors, or support groups provides essential emotional nourishment and practical advice. These connections offer perspective and affirmation, creating a shared strength that enhances individual resilience. The mutual exchange of support and encouragement fosters environments where resilience can thrive, reinforcing the belief that challenges can be overcome through collective effort. By weaving these strategies into the fabric of daily life, individuals cultivate an inner resilience that empowers them to navigate life's inevitable challenges with confidence and grace. The journey to building resilience is one of continual growth and transformation, where each experience contributes to a profound understanding of one's capabilities and strengths.

This holistic integration of connection, wellness, healthy thinking, and meaning forms the bedrock upon which personal empowerment and self-discovery are built, propelling individuals toward their fullest potential with courage and resilience.

Fostering Emotional Intelligence

Fostering emotional intelligence (EI) is a transformative endeavor that significantly enhances an individual's capacity for resilience. Emotional intelligence, the ability to recognize, understand, and manage emotions effectively, provides a robust framework for navigating life's challenges with grace and poise. High EI not only equips individuals to handle personal and professional adversities but also empowers them to cultivate enduring relationships and supportive networks that bolster resilience.

At the heart of emotional intelligence lies self-awareness, the ability to identify and comprehend one's own emotions and their impact on decisions and behaviors. Self-awareness serves as a critical foundation, enabling individuals to gain insight into their emotional processes and triggers. Practices such as mindfulness and journaling enhance this awareness by encouraging reflection and introspection. Mindfulness fosters a present-moment focus, allowing individuals to observe their thoughts and feelings without judgment. Journaling provides a tangible record of emotional patterns, promoting clarity and self-understanding.

Self-regulation is another cornerstone of emotional intelligence, facilitating the management of emotional responses, particularly in adversity. This component involves recognizing emotional triggers and implementing strategies to manage reactions thoughtfully. Adopting a "pause, step back, and assess" approach allows individuals to interrupt impulsive responses, paving the way for measured and reflective decision-making. By cultivating self-regulation, individuals develop a calm, composed demeanor that aids in navigating stress and fluctuations of daily life.

Motivation, rooted in emotional intelligence, acts as a driving force that propels individuals forward, even in the face of challenges. It encompasses setting meaningful goals, exploring personal passions, and visualizing the impact of one's actions. Motivation provides direction and purpose, stabilizing individuals amidst life's uncertainties. A strong sense of motivation encourages perseverance and resilience, allowing individuals to overcome setbacks with determination and resilience.

Empathy represents a vital component of emotional intelligence, encompassing both self-compassion and an understanding of others. Empathetic individuals can navigate complex social situations smoothly, fostering strong, supportive relationships that are crucial for resilience. Empathy enhances the ability to connect with others on a deeper level, building a sense of community and belonging. It encourages individuals to respond to others with kindness and understanding, reinforcing the social fabric that supports personal and collective resilience.

Social skills, including effective communication and relationship-building, are essential elements of emotional intelligence. These skills facilitate the creation of robust support networks, providing emotional sustenance during challenging times. Techniques such as open-ended questioning encourage deeper connections and meaningful dialogues. By honing social skills, individuals can maintain strong relationships that offer comfort and guidance, essential components of a resilient life.

Individuals with high emotional intelligence are more likely to experience positive emotions, forge healthier relationships, and enjoy overall well-being. These attributes collectively enhance the ability to cope with adversity, fostering increased resilience. Positive emotions act as a buffer against stress, promoting adaptive coping mechanisms and reinforcing a growth-oriented mindset. The strong relationships cultivated through high EI provide a network of support and encouragement, mitigating the impact of life's challenges.

Conversely, low emotional intelligence poses significant challenges to resilience. Individuals who struggle with self-regulation may exhibit impulsive behaviors and poor decision-making, exacerbating stress and complicating personal and professional relationships. Low EI often correlates with negative emotional states, relationship difficulties, and diminished mental health, all of which undermine resilience. Addressing these challenges involves developing the skills and awareness necessary to enhance emotional intelligence and resilience.

Practical strategies for fostering emotional intelligence encompass mindfulness, journaling, and techniques such as the "pause, step back and assess" approach. Mindfulness encourages individuals to engage with their emotions openly, fostering self-awareness and reducing reactivity. Journaling provides an outlet for emotional exploration and serves as a reflective practice that deepens understanding. The "pause, step back, and assess" technique interrupts automatic reactions, encouraging deliberate consideration and emotional regulation.

Building strong relationships and setting achievable goals further nurture emotional intelligence and resilience. By prioritizing relationships that offer mutual support and understanding, individuals cultivate a network that reinforces emotional well-being. Setting clear, attainable goals provides motivation and direction, reinforcing positive emotions and a sense of accomplishment. Together, these strategies offer a roadmap for developing emotional intelligence and resilience, enriching the journey of personal empowerment and self-discovery.

Through the integration of these components and strategies, individuals enhance their capability to navigate emotional landscapes with confidence and insight. Emotional intelligence and resilience form a synergistic partnership, where each reinforces the other in a powerful cycle of growth and adaptation. By embracing this journey, individuals unlock their potential for resilience, fostering a life of fulfillment, balance, and profound personal empowerment.

Creating a Supportive Network

Creating a supportive network is a vital component of cultivating inner resilience and navigating the ups and downs of life with fortitude and ease. In a world where stress and challenges are inevitable, having a strong social foundation provides the emotional sustenance and perspective needed to weather any storm. Building these networks is not just about amassing social connections but about nurturing meaningful relationships that offer mutual support, understanding, and encouragement.

At the heart of a supportive network lies the importance of strong relationships. Connection with others forms the backbone of emotional support and fosters a sense of belonging. Regularly engaging with loved ones—through sharing experiences, offering support, and participating in shared activities—strengthens these bonds. These interactions create safe spaces where individuals can express themselves openly, exchange ideas, and provide mutual encouragement. The strength of these bonds significantly fortifies resilience, enabling individuals to face life's hurdles with collective strength.

The quality of interactions within a support network often holds more significance than the sheer number of connections. High-quality interactions are characterized by authenticity, empathy, and deep engagement. By participating in shared activities, individuals can foster meaningful connections that are rich in support and understanding. Whether through engaging in communal hobbies, participating in family gatherings, or simply having deep conversations, the essence of these connections lies in the value and depth they bring to one's life.

A robust support network is not limited to friends and family; it can be expanded through strategic actions. Surrounding oneself with trusted friends, family, or support groups forms the core of this network, providing emotional anchors during challenging times. Joining clubs, volunteering, or participating in support groups opens doors to new relationships that broaden the spectrum of support. These activities encourage individuals to meet like-minded people, fostering connections based on shared interests and common goals. Investing in these areas allows the formation of a network that bolsters resilience through emotional and practical support.

In addition to personal networks, seeking professional help enhances the depth of support available. Therapists, coaches, and counselors bring expertise that helps individuals understand emotional patterns, develop coping strategies, and clarify personal goals. Professional guidance enriches the support network, providing insights and tools that empower individuals to manage emotions effectively and navigate life's complexities with confidence. Engaging with professionals offers a structured avenue for personal growth, complementing the emotional reinforcement received from personal relationships.

Community engagement serves as a powerful catalyst for building a supportive network. Participating in local clubs or volunteering creates opportunities to forge meaningful connections and nurture a sense of community. These engagements foster collective resilience, as individuals come together to address community needs, celebrate successes, and provide collective support. Community involvement gives individuals a sense of purpose and belonging, reinforcing their role within a network that is greater than themselves.

Integral to developing a supportive network is the practice of self-compassion. Embracing vulnerabilities with kindness allows individuals to approach challenges without shame.

Self-compassion involves treating oneself with the same understanding and care one would offer to a friend. By creating a non-judgmental space for self-reflection, individuals can share experiences and emotions with awareness and acceptance, building emotional self-reliance. This internal support enhances external networks, as self-compassionate individuals are better equipped to engage empathetically with others.

Practicing self-compassion feeds into the broader support network by fostering a culture of empathy and acceptance. When individuals demonstrate understanding and kindness toward their own experiences, they naturally extend these qualities to their interactions with others. This creates a supportive network characterized by mutual respect and authentic connection, where people feel safe sharing their stories and challenges.

Integrating these strategies into daily life builds a resilient support network capable of enhancing inner fortitude and well-being. By consciously investing in relationships and engaging with communities, individuals solidify a foundation that cushions them from life's adversities. A strong support network acts as a buffer against stress, offering diverse perspectives and encouragement that promote emotional resilience.

This network enriches personal growth, providing a platform for sharing knowledge, resources, and experiences that contribute to personal empowerment. Encouragement from a supportive network inspires individuals to pursue personal goals and embrace self-discovery, as the collective wisdom and support of the group uplift individual aspirations.

The journey to creating a supportive network is one of intentional cultivation and meaningful engagement. It requires dedication to nurturing relationships and a commitment to being both a source and recipient of support. As individuals build these networks, they contribute to a dynamic and supportive ecosystem, where the combined strength and wisdom of the group amplify individual resilience. Through this interconnected web of support, life's challenges become shared experiences, navigated with collaboration and strength. This collective resilience transforms personal growth into a shared journey, elevating both the individual and the community in a harmonious dance of empowerment and discovery.

CHAPTER 8: Finding Balance in a Chaotic World

Life Design Principles

Life Design Principles offer a powerful framework for individuals seeking to find balance and empowerment amidst the chaos of modern life.

By providing a structured approach to navigating personal and professional challenges, these principles empower individuals to align their actions with their core values and aspirations, thereby fostering a life of fulfillment and purpose.

Acceptance and presence are foundational to Life Design. Embracing the present involves recognizing and accepting one's current circumstances, which can include a variety of career aspirations and life goals. This principle calls for a growth mindset, allowing individuals to remain open to new experiences and perspectives. By accepting where we are now, we open ourselves to the possibilities of change and growth and foster resilience against the challenges life may throw our way.

Understanding oneself with empathy is vital in building a balanced life. This involves deep self-reflection to uncover desires, strengths, and vulnerabilities, allowing for informed decision-making regarding life's pathways. Empathy extends beyond self-evaluation; it also includes considering the perspectives and experiences of others. This broader understanding helps individuals make decisions that are not only self-serving but also harmonious with the needs and feelings of those around them. Cultivating a profound self-awareness is instrumental in designing a life that is genuinely reflective of personal values and ambitions.

Life Design is about discovery and clarification of true interests and strengths. Various exercises and assessments assist individuals in exploring a broad spectrum of possibilities, helping clarify what genuinely matters to them. This process involves identifying core values and priorities that guide meaningful life choices. Clarification brings focus, helping individuals filter opportunities that align with their unique vision of a fulfilling life. The clarity achieved through this principle also provides a roadmap for personal and professional growth, ensuring that each step taken is purposeful.

The development of critical life skills is central to the Life Design approach. Skills such as problem-solving, creativity, empathy, and resilience are not only essential for making meaningful choices but also for navigating the inherent uncertainties of life. These skills are cultivated through an iterative process of experiential learning and reflection, reinforcing the individual's ability to adapt to new challenges. This empowerment comes from knowing that, regardless of circumstances, one possesses the tools to craft a path forward.

Real-world experience is invaluable in the Life Design journey. Engaging in internships, volunteering, and other hands-on activities provides direct exposure to potential career paths and validates or refines one's interests. Such experiences offer critical insights that cannot be obtained through theoretical exploration alone. This direct engagement with the world enhances understanding and confidence, equipping individuals to make informed career and life decisions.

Building connections and networks is another key element of Life Design. Creating relationships with professionals in fields of interest not only provides insider knowledge but also forms a support system that can guide and influence career paths. Networks offer opportunities for mentorship, collaboration, and opportunity discovery, contributing significantly to both personal and professional growth. The strength of these connections often determines the ease with which individuals can transition through various stages of their careers.

Implementing an evolving life plan ensures that Life Design remains dynamic and responsive to changes in circumstances and aspirations. This approach encourages continuous reflection, adaptation, and action toward a fulfilling, purpose-driven life. Regularly revisiting and revising the life plan maintains alignment with personal growth and external changes, ensuring that individuals remain on a path that is both relevant and inspiring.

Recent developments highlight the increasing integration of Life Design principles in educational settings. Colleges and universities recognize the value of such frameworks in enhancing student well-being and academic pursuits, and in preparing students for future challenges. Life Design workshops and retreats, such as the *2025* Life Design Retreat at NYU, are instrumental in helping participants navigate critical transition moments and choose meaningful next steps. These educational initiatives underscore the relevance of Life Design principles in supporting individuals through periods of change.

Life Design Principles offer a comprehensive guide for individuals aiming to navigate the complexities of modern life with intentionality and grace. By integrating these principles into daily practice, individuals cultivate a balanced lifestyle that empowers them to pursue meaningful careers and personal growth. This structured yet flexible approach equips individuals with the mindset and tools needed to thrive, providing a foundation for sustained personal empowerment and self-discovery. As each principle is embraced, individuals move closer to realizing a life of alignment, balance, and profound personal fulfillment.

Time Management Strategies

Effective time management is foundational in finding balance amidst the chaos of modern life. In *2025*, the landscape of time management has evolved significantly, influenced by technological advancements and innovative strategies that enhance productivity, reduce stress, and foster personal empowerment.

Leveraging technology is a cornerstone of modern time management. Innovative tools such as project management software, AI-driven scheduling assistants, and collaborative platforms offer unprecedented support in streamlining workflows and automating routine tasks. By reducing time spent on administrative duties and improving team alignment, these technologies enhance overall efficiency. Integrating these tools with existing work applications minimizes the time lost in transitioning between platforms, allowing individuals to focus more energy on creative and complex tasks that demand attention.

Time management techniques provide structured approaches to balancing responsibilities effectively. Timeboxing is a technique that designates specific periods for completing tasks, helping individuals stay focused and goal-oriented. By dedicating set intervals for work, timeboxing minimizes procrastination and encapsulates work within defined boundaries, creating a psychological commitment to task completion.

The Pomodoro Technique has gained popularity for its ability to enhance productivity and focus through interval work sessions. By working intensely for a predetermined period, traditionally *25* minutes, followed by a short break, individuals can maintain high levels of concentration without succumbing to burnout. This cyclic approach supports sustained productivity and keeps the mind fresh throughout the day.

The Eisenhower Matrix is another powerful tool that assists in prioritizing tasks based on urgency and importance. By categorizing tasks into quadrants—urgent and important, important but not urgent, urgent but not important, and neither urgent nor important—individuals can focus on critical tasks first, ensuring that essential duties are addressed in a timely manner. This strategic prioritization prevents the escalation of urgent tasks into emergencies, freeing up mental space for strategic planning and innovation.

Embracing single tasking over multitasking has been shown to significantly boost efficiency and reduce overwhelm. In contrast to multitasking, which divides attention, single tasking involves focusing on one task at a time, leading to higher quality outcomes and greater fulfillment in work. This approach encourages deep work, where concentration and cognitive energy are wholly dedicated to the task at hand, fostering both speed and quality in task execution.

Scheduling and prioritization play critical roles in effective time management. Treating important tasks as non-negotiable commitments involves scheduling them just as one would for pivotal meetings or appointments. This approach emphasizes the value of one's goals and ensures they receive the attention and energy they deserve. Breaking larger tasks into smaller, manageable pieces and assigning dedicated time blocks for these tasks helps maintain focus and momentum.

Batching tasks, such as checking emails, into scheduled windows can prevent constant interruptions, improving time control and reducing stress.

Remote work presents unique challenges that require tailored strategies for success. Agile time management practices become essential in remote settings, where blending home and work life can blur boundaries. Utilizing technological tools to manage tasks effectively and regularly adjusting time blocks based on feedback ensures that task lists remain relevant and achievable. This proactive adaptation fosters a robust work-life balance, essential for maintaining motivation and productivity in a non-traditional work environment.

Achieving work-life balance requires setting clear boundaries between work tasks and personal time. Protecting designated work periods allows for focused, uninterrupted effort, while also ensuring personal and family commitments are honored. Taking regular breaks throughout the workday helps sustain energy levels and focus while preventing burnout. The deliberate separation of work and personal time cultivates a balanced lifestyle, where individuals can pursue both professional ambitions and personal interests with vitality and purpose.

Collectively, these time management strategies empower individuals to navigate their lives with greater ease and control. By managing time effectively, individuals reduce stress, enhance productivity, and cultivate a sense of balance that supports personal empowerment and self-discovery. In a world where demands on time continue to increase, mastering these strategies equips individuals to thrive amidst chaos, creating space for growth, creativity, and fulfillment in all areas of life. By integrating these principles into daily routines, individuals set a foundation for a more organized, productive, and satisfied existence, allowing them to fully embrace the opportunities and challenges life presents.

Nurturing Healthy Relationships

Nurturing healthy relationships is integral to finding balance in an increasingly chaotic world. At the heart of any thriving relationship lies the ability to connect deeply and communicate effectively. This foundation allows individuals to support each other's personal growth while moving towards shared aspirations. By understanding and implementing key strategies for relationship nurturing, individuals can foster connections that enrich their lives and contribute to personal empowerment and self-discovery.

Prioritizing communication serves as the cornerstone of healthy relationships. Effective communication means more than exchanging words; it involves creating a safe and open environment where all parties feel comfortable sharing thoughts and feelings without facing judgment or defensiveness. Active listening plays a crucial role in this exchange, as it enables partners to truly hear and understand one another, fostering emotional intimacy. Practicing empathy—the ability to perceive and reflect the feelings of others—deepens the quality of communication, helping to resolve conflicts amicably and strengthen relational bonds.

Growth and development are hallmarks of healthy relationships, characterized by their dynamic and evolving nature. Encouraging personal and shared growth is essential to sustaining a relationship's vitality. Supporting each partner's passions and interests allows for individual fulfillment, bringing fresh perspectives and energy into the relationship. Simultaneously, sharing goals and development projects as a couple creates a sense of unity and purpose. This mutual support acts as a catalyst for both personal and relational enrichment, reinforcing the bond that underlies the partnership.

In the hustle and bustle of daily life, it's easy to overlook the need for regular relationship maintenance. Establishing rituals for connection can counteract this tendency, providing structured opportunities for partners to reconnect and reaffirm their commitment to one another. These rituals need not be elaborate; they can range from weekly date nights to simple daily check-ins. Such dedicated time allows for deeper discussions about emotional states, needs, and desires, ensuring that both partners feel heard and valued. By consistently nurturing these moments, couples can keep their relationship aligned with their evolving needs and circumstances.

Reflecting on the past and setting shared goals for the future fortifies relationships against the challenges of time and change. Periodic reflection encourages couples to identify areas for improvement and acknowledge achievements, providing a framework for growth and continuity. By developing a shared vision for the future, including clear and actionable goals, partners ensure they are moving in tandem towards common aspirations. This intentional approach helps cement a strong foundation for the relationship, promoting resilience and adaptability.

Being proactive and intentional about relationships means actively engaging in their maintenance rather than allowing them to drift into autopilot mode. This involves making a conscious effort to reach out, prioritize, and assess how relationships align with personal values. Intentionality in relationships cultivates a satisfying and fulfilling connection, as it fosters awareness and action tailored to the needs and desires of all involved. Regularly taking stock of relationships provides the opportunity to recalibrate and refresh, ensuring they remain a source of support and happiness.

Intentional communication—characterized by empathy, kindness, and timely resolution of issues—is vital for building trust and intimacy in relationships. This type of communication demands honesty and openness, allowing space for partners to voice concerns and celebrate joys alike. Attending to issues promptly prevents resentment from building and promotes a culture of understanding and patience. By prioritizing intentional communication, individuals can navigate the unpredictability of modern life while maintaining strong, healthy relationships.

By incorporating these practices into their relationships, individuals can cultivate environments of balanced support and nurturing. These relationships, in turn, bolster personal empowerment and self-discovery, providing a stable platform from which individuals can explore and embrace the complexities of life. As each partner grows within the relationship, the partnership itself evolves, reflecting a dynamic balance of individual growth and mutual aspiration.

Effective communication, mutual support in personal growth, consistent connection rituals, reflective goal-setting, proactive engagement, and intentional dialogue form the bedrock of thriving relationships that nurture participants and withstand stressors. These elements collectively create an enriching and resilient partnership, where both individuals feel valued and empowered to pursue their full potential. As such, nurturing healthy relationships is not solely about maintaining harmony but is a powerful contributor to a fulfilling and empowered life.

Through these concerted efforts in relationship building, individuals learn to share their journeys with others, creating bonds that enhance resilience and enrich life's tapestry. A supportive, intentional partnership becomes a source of strength and inspiration, empowering both individuals to flourish even amidst life's chaos. This nurturing process—that of building and maintaining vibrant, healthy relationships—aligns closely with the essence of personal empowerment and the quest for a balanced, meaningful existence.

CHAPTER 9: Harnessing the Power of Intuition

Trusting Your Gut Feelings

Trusting your gut feelings is an integral facet of navigating the complexities of modern life. Intuition—those immediate, almost instinctual feelings or hunches—serves as an invaluable tool in decision-making, innovation, and handling uncertainty. As society speeds forward, intuition bridges the gap between analytical thinking and the vast unconscious processing of information, providing a holistic lens through which to view the world. Intuition is gaining recognition as more than just an abstract or mystical idea. Emerging research validates intuition as a significant player in decision-making processes. Studies involving notable figures, including Nobel laureates, illustrate how intuition can connect disparate ideas and catalyze groundbreaking innovations. The human brain processes countless pieces of information unconsciously, and intuition enables the swift synthesis of this data, often reaching conclusions more rapidly than deliberate, conscious thought.

Harnessing the power of intuition requires cultivating a deep connection with oneself, allowing individuals to access and trust their inner wisdom. Mindfulness practices such as meditation, creative visualization, and engaging in artistic endeavors enhance self-awareness and provide the space to silently converse with one's intuitive self. Mindful practices encourage the quiet that intuition needs to speak, nurturing the ability to discern subtle cues and insights that might otherwise remain buried under the noise of everyday life.

Reflecting on past experiences can bolster confidence in intuitive decision-making. By revisiting instances where following one's gut led to positive outcomes, individuals build a retrospective understanding of how intuition has served them well. These reflections offer reassurance of intuition’s efficacy and reinforce trust in one's internal guidance system. Through this self-reflection, the connection to intuition is strengthened, reassuring individuals that their instincts often guide them correctly.

Balancing intuition with rational analysis is crucial for well-rounded decision-making. While intuition offers quick insights, rational analysis provides a structured approach that can validate or refine these initial inclinations. This synergistic approach ensures that decisions are rooted in both emotional intelligence and logical reasoning. In situations where emotions run high or stakes are significant, balancing gut feelings with objective analysis minimizes the risk of impulsive decisions that might overlook critical aspects.

In uncertain and fast-paced environments, intuition becomes particularly advantageous. It allows individuals to make decisions aligned with their core values and deepest instincts, offering a compass when logic alone may falter. Intuition provides a sense of alignment and integrity that rational thought might at times miss, particularly when the landscape is muddled with complexity or ambiguity. However, systematic thinking can sometimes yield more empathically accurate results, underscoring the importance of embracing a balanced approach. Personal empowerment and self-discovery are enriched through trusting one's gut feelings. Intuition guides individuals toward choices and paths that resonate with their true selves, fostering authenticity and courage.

By attuning to intuition, individuals can sharply focus on stress reduction, honing in on what truly matters while situations. This navigating high-pressure centeredness enhances leadership capabilities and personal growth, cultivating a resilience that radiates from within.

The practical application of intuition spans various facets of life and work. In leadership, intuition aids in anticipating future trends or market shifts that are not immediately visible through data alone. In personal life, it guides individuals toward relationships and environments that nurture their well-being. Understanding the importance of intuition and learning to trust it can lead to more fulfilling and purposeful living.

Integrating intuition into daily decision-making practices encourages a harmonious balance of heart and mind. Cultivating this balance pays dividends in creativity, problem-solving, and insightfulness, empowering individuals to act with confidence and assurance. Trust in intuition catalyzes a dynamic synergy between the known and unknown, allowing individuals to navigate the ever-evolving landscape of modern life with clarity and conviction.

Acknowledging the scientific validation of intuition elevates its standing in the realm of decision-making. It stands as a credible and essential element that complements cognitive processes, enabling individuals to make comprehensive and informed choices. This recognition propels intuition from the shadows of skepticism into a guiding force that integrates seamlessly with fact-based reasoning.

In the pursuit of personal empowerment and self-discovery, intuition serves as an unwavering guide, illuminating paths not yet trodden and igniting the courage to forge new ones. By embracing intuition, individuals open themselves to a world where instinctual wisdom merges with intellectual analysis, leading to more resilient and adaptive decision-making frameworks.

To trust one's gut is to cultivate a relationship with the self that honors both understanding and instinct. Empowered by intuition, individuals navigate their lives with enriched perspectives and renewed vigor, transcending the conventional limitations of knowledge and perception. As individuals continue to explore and harness this intrinsic force, they journey toward a deeper alignment with their inner selves and an expanded potential for growth and innovation. This journey, marked by the interplay of intuition and reason, underpins the essence of transformative personal empowerment.

Intuitive Decision Making

Intuitive decision-making represents a fascinating intersection between instinct and intellect, offering a nuanced approach to navigating the complexities of modern life. At its core, intuition is a rapid, non-conscious process that synthesizes vast and diverse data into simple, actionable insights. Unlike the methodical pace of analytic reasoning, intuition provides immediate clarity, propelling decision-makers through nuanced environments with instinctual ease.

The duality of decision-making approaches underscores the complementary nature of intuition and systematic methods. Intuition serves as a guiding force, particularly when time is constrained or when navigating ambiguous terrain.

In agriculture, for example, farmers often rely on intuition as a "decision-making assistant" that reconciles gut feelings with seasonal patterns, weather conditions, and other environmental signals. This instinctual guidance plays a crucial role in beginning and end stages of the analytical process, where exhaustive data collection might be impractical or impossible. The reliance on instincts in such contexts emphasizes the richness of experiential knowledge, where years of subtle learning inform swift judgments.

Contrastingly, the field of "choice engineering" introduces precision into decision-making using mathematical models and optimization techniques. This approach, grounded in rigorous quantification, offers structured pathways through complex decisions. The emergence of choice engineering suggests that mathematical models might outperform intuitive judgments by mitigating cognitive biases and ensuring consistent decision quality. Yet, rather than exist as opposing forces, choice engineering and intuition can converge, creating a harmonious balance that capitalizes on both spontaneity and structure.

Intuition's value lies in its ability to enhance creativity and foster innovation. By facilitating novel connections, it encourages thinking beyond conventional paradigms, sparking insights that drive originality and progress. This capability is crucial in industries requiring imaginative problem-solving, such as technology and design. Indeed, intuition can transform the intangible into the tangible; it accesses latent potentials that systematic thought alone might overlook. For regenerative farmers, intuition aligns with the 'voice of reason,' as they tactfully blend experience and instinct to guide sustainable practices.

Cultural and contextual factors influence preferences for intuitive versus deliberative decision-making. Cultural backgrounds shape the degree of trust placed in intuition, with variations observed across geographic regions and professional domains. A study in the public sector reveals how cultural context affects the reliance on intuitive and affective decision-making, with significant differences noted across countries. These variations highlight the contextual nature of decision-making styles, where culture and experience blend to determine individual or collective preference for intuitive or methodical processes.

Integrating intuitive insights with systematic methods, as suggested by choice engineering, enhances decision-making efficacy.

This integration offers a balanced model that marries the agility of intuition with the precision of mathematical analysis, optimizing outcomes through comprehensive strategies. By doing so, individuals can employ a structured yet flexible approach that encompasses the best of both worlds, facilitating ethically sound and contextually appropriate decisions. The cohesion of these methods fosters a synergy that propels strategic innovation and empowerment.

While much is understood about the mechanics of logical reasoning, empirical research on intuition remains sparse and fragmented. The nuanced role of intuition in decision-making warrants further exploration to unveil its depth and breadth across diverse contexts. Investigating intuition's influence on personal and professional choices could yield insights that transcend current conceptions, broadening the lens through which we view instinctual processes.

Cultivating intuitive skills can enhance one's capacity for decision-making. responsive and adaptive Mindfulness practices, reflective exercises, and creative pursuits allow individuals to tune into their inner compass, heightening awareness and trust in gut feelings. Simultaneously, grounding intuitive judgments in systematic reasoning mitigates the risk of impulsivity, reinforcing confidence in balanced decisions.

Empowered decision-making arises from integrating intuition with analysis, enabling informed and agile responses to life's varied demands. This dual approach caters both to the emotional and rational facets of the human psyche, reflecting a comprehensive understanding that fosters personal and professional growth. As individuals harness their intuitive capabilities, they encounter newfound clarity and focus in decisions, fostering an alignment between impulse and insight.

In today's rapidly evolving world, cultivating the ability to trust and channel intuition becomes an integral aspect of self-discovery and empowerment. Intuitive decision-making is not a dismissal of logic, but a complementary force that enriches intellectual exploration and enhances emotional intelligence. As the exploration of intuition continues, it stands poised to play an increasingly significant role in shaping innovative pathways through the intricacies of modern existence, marrying the dynamic expression of instinct with the steadfastness of analytical precision. Such an approach imbues decisions with the wisdom of intuition while anchoring them in the clarity of reason, a testament to the symbiotic power of insight and intellect.

Cultivating Creative Insights

Cultivating creative insights through the lens of intuition offers a transformative pathway to personal empowerment and self-discovery. Intuition, often described as a powerful inner guide, transcends the limitations of linear and logical thought processes by tapping into a higher creative consciousness. This faculty enables individuals to access a reservoir of knowledge and imagination that can drive innovation and inspire original thought.

Harnessing intuition involves engaging with the subconscious mind and allowing it to influence creative endeavors. Practices such as mindfulness, achieving a flow state, and connecting with higher intelligence underscore the development of intuitive insight. These methods encourage a deep inner stillness that opens the door to intuition, allowing creativity to flow unhindered by the usual constraints of critical reasoning. Within this expansive mental space, individuals can discover novel solutions, fresh perspectives, and imaginative ideas that fuel artistic and intellectual pursuits.

The integration of cutting-edge technologies further enhances the capacity for creative collaboration in the modern era. In *2025*, creative teams leverage advanced digital tools to streamline collaboration, ensuring that innovative ideas are efficiently transformed into reality. Technologies enable more nuanced expressions of creativity, allowing for personalized and authentic outputs that resonate with diverse audiences. By pushing the boundaries of traditional creative processes, technology empowers artists and thinkers to achieve unprecedented levels of quality and speed in their work, maximizing the impact of creative intuition.

A shift towards personalized and flexible approaches in creative processes aligns with nurturing intuition. Embracing intentions over rigid goals invites flexibility in creative pursuits, promoting self-compassion and acknowledging the non-linear nature of the creative journey. This approach emphasizes consistent, intentional steps, allowing for the natural ebb and flow of inspiration and productivity. In valuing curiosity, continuous learning, and small projects, individuals foster an environment where creativity thrives organically, free from the pressure of external expectations and perfectionism.

Practical techniques for cultivating intuition draw from both ancient traditions and modern innovations. Utilizing creativity, metaphor, and observational skills to enhance intuitive fluency empowers individuals to reclaim their inner knowing. This practice heightens problem-solving abilities and effectively applies intuitive insights across various facets of life. By creating a personalized approach to intuition, individuals tailor these techniques to fit their unique contexts, enhancing their ability to leverage intuitive insights in personal and professional domains.

The significance of mindfulness and flow state in realizing intuitive potential cannot be overstated. Mindfulness engenders a heightened state of awareness, where moment-to-moment experiences are honored and observed without judgment. This awareness paves the way for intuitive understanding, as the mind becomes attuned to subtle cues and inspirations. Achieving a flow state—a condition where one is fully immersed and engaged in an activity—amplifies access to subconscious ideas, facilitating a seamless connection with creative intuition that enhances output and problem-solving capabilities.

This multifaceted approach to cultivating creative insights marries intuition with technological tools and adaptable strategies, crafting a comprehensive framework for fostering artistic and analytical innovation. By combining these methods, individuals unlock pathways of intuition that empower them to explore new dimensions of creativity and self-expression.

In the practice of cultivating creative insights, fully embracing intuition offers liberating possibilities. It equips individuals with the confidence to transcend conventional thinking and traverse unexplored territories of thought. Intuitive insight acts as a beacon, illuminating paths toward original solutions and groundbreaking ideas that redefine creative landscapes.

Embracing intuition as a central tenet in the creative process acknowledges the complexity and depth of human cognition. By integrating intuition into our daily lives, we can harness its transformative potential, expanding our capacity for both personal growth and collective innovation. The balance between instinctive knowledge and technological advancement creates fertile ground for creativity to flourish in diverse and impactful ways, leading to enriched experiences and profound insights.

Intuition's role in creativity and insight invites us to look beyond the obvious, to trust our inner voice, and to act with conviction even in the absence of complete evidence. This trust nurtures an empowered relationship with oneself, cultivating an environment where creativity is not only expressed but celebrated as a vital aspect of human existence. As individuals refine their connection to intuition, they contribute to a broader renaissance of creativity—a transformation that impacts not just personal empowerment, but the collective evolution of society as well.

CHAPTER 10: Sustaining Your Personal Growth Journey

Setting Long-Term Goals

Setting long-term goals is an empowering process that acts as a guiding compass on the journey of personal growth. It provides a structured path that aligns with an individual's core values and aspirations, ensuring that each step taken contributes to the broader narrative of self-discovery and empowerment. In the chaos of daily life, long-term goals serve as anchors that stabilize and signify direction, fostering resilience and purpose.

The foundational framework for effective long-term goal-setting is the SMART criteria. This method outlines that goals should be Specific, Measurable, Attainable, Relevant, and Time-bound. The specificity of a goal ensures clarity, establishing a well-defined target. For instance, transforming a vague desire like "I want to become healthier" into a SMART goal, such as "I will engage in *30* minutes of cardiovascular exercise, three times a week, for the next six months to improve my health," provides a concrete roadmap. This specificity is crucial in creating actionable steps that are not only clear but also practical.

Measurability provides a way to track progress, serving as a metric for success. It transforms abstract ambitions into tangible outcomes. Attainability ensures goals are realistic and within reach, fostering motivation rather than intimidation. Relevance aligns the goal with broader life objectives and personal values, underscoring the importance of the pursuit in the grand scheme of personal development. Lastly, having a time-bound aspect instills urgency and commitment, framing the endeavor within a realistic timeline that encourages consistent effort.

Integral to setting meaningful goals is self-reflection, a practice that involves delving into personal strengths, weaknesses, and passions. This introspection reveals core values, guiding the alignment of goals with an individual's authentic ethos. By asking questions such as "What activities bring me joy?" or "What changes do I seek in my life?" individuals can set goals that resonate deeply, fueling intrinsic motivation. This alignment is vital, as it ensures that the pursuit of goals contributes not only to external achievements but also to internal fulfillment and satisfaction.

Breaking down long-term goals into smaller, manageable objectives transforms grand visions into achievable milestones. This approach mitigates overwhelm, distributing the intensity of the task across a continuum of progress. For example, if one's objective is to write a book, setting short-term goals like drafting a set number of pages weekly or completing chapters by specific dates provides structure and focus. These sub-goals serve as stepping stones, each one celebrating progress and reinforcing the commitment to the longer journey.

Flexibility is a crucial attribute in goal-setting, recognizing that life's dynamism often necessitates adjustments. Circumstances evolve, and being open to modifying goals or strategies ensures that progress persists despite changing conditions. Tools such as quarterly evaluations or weekly check-ins can track development and recalibrate efforts to stay aligned with primary objectives. This adaptability prevents stagnation and sustains momentum, allowing for responsive growth in the face of unforeseen challenges.

Documenting goals by writing them down instills a sense of accountability and commitment. Research underscores that the mere act of recording goals can significantly increase the likelihood of accomplishing them. Sharing these goals with a friend, mentor, or coach introduces a level of external accountability, offering support and encouragement along the way. This interaction enriches the goal-setting process, as fellow collaborators or mentors may offer insights or strategies that enhance the journey.

Examples of enriching long-term goals encompass a diverse array of pursuits, all designed to enhance personal growth and life satisfaction. Whether it's acquiring a new language, embarking on travel adventures, honing time management skills, dedicating attention to self-care, or cultivating proficiency in public speaking, these goals reflect a dedication to self-improvement and holistic development. Each goal should be uniquely tailored, reflecting personal aspirations and values, to ensure that they contribute meaningfully to empowerment and self-discovery.

In integrating these principles and strategies, individuals craft a robust and purposeful approach to achieving their long-term goals. This process not only facilitates the realization of specific objectives but also transforms the very act of pursuing goals into an enriching journey. It empowers individuals to navigate life's complexities with assurance and determination, understanding that each milestone offers lessons and opportunities for growth.

The pursuit and attainment of long-term goals can be likened to an evolving narrative, where each goal accomplished denotes a chapter in the larger story of life. This pursuit instills a sense of purpose and progress, creating a tapestry woven with intricate patterns of experience and knowledge.

By maintaining focus and adhering to structured, yet adaptable, strategies, individuals can achieve their aspirations while fostering a profound connection with themselves.

Ultimately, setting long-term goals aligns with the overarching desire for personal empowerment and self-discovery. It challenges individuals to stretch beyond their comfort zones, engage with their deepest desires, and harness their inner force to effect meaningful change. The clarity and commitment fostered by well-defined goals not only enhance personal growth but illuminate the path toward a future of possibility and fulfillment. Each goal achieved reflects the transformative power of intentionality and dedication, guiding individuals toward a life rich with purpose, achievement, and inner strength.

Evaluating Your Progress

Evaluating your progress is a vital aspect of any personal growth journey, serving as a checkpoint that provides clarity and direction. This reflective practice enables individuals to gauge their progress, validate their efforts, and recalibrate their goals if necessary. It ensures that growth is intentional and aligned with personal aspirations and values, thereby sustaining momentum on the path of self-discovery and empowerment.

Regular self-assessment and reflection are foundational to understanding one's current standing in relation to personal objectives. This process involves a candid examination of life changes, an evaluation of the fulfillment these changes provide, and an exploration of future learning interests. By assessing how time is spent and what aspects of life bring joy or dissatisfaction, individuals can align their daily actions with overarching goals. This alignment nurtures a sense of purpose and direction, invigorating the pursuit of continued growth.

Conducting a holistic assessment of strengths and weaknesses enhances self-awareness and identifies areas for improvement. Incorporating feedback from trusted friends, family, and professional contacts offers a comprehensive perspective that personal reflection alone might miss. Tools like 360-degree feedback help gather insights from multiple angles, highlighting potential reinforcing blind spots and self-development areas. This comprehensive assessment empowers individuals to leverage their strengths and address any weaknesses, fostering a balanced approach to personal growth.

Setting and achieving clear, actionable goals across various life dimensions solidifies the foundation for sustained progress. Goals should be specific and measurable, spanning areas such as physical well-being, emotional intelligence, career advancement, and relationships. Breaking larger goals into smaller, manageable steps facilitates continuous progress. For instance, enhancing physical health might involve setting weekly exercise targets and dietary plans, while cultivating emotional intelligence could focus on mindfulness practices and improved communication skills.

The use of tools and resources is instrumental in supporting personal growth and evaluating progress. Personality assessments and growth questionnaires provide insights into personal tendencies and areas for growth. Digital applications like MyFitnessPal or Fitbit offer practical ways to track health and fitness progress, while curated reading lists and online guides furnish actionable insights for development across other life areas. Engaging with these resources enriches one's growth journey, providing both guidance and structure.

Continuous improvement is an ongoing pursuit that involves regularly measuring growth against established goals. This can be achieved through periodic self-evaluations and by seeking external feedback. By regularly updating and refining personal development plans, individuals maintain a dynamic and responsive approach to growth.

This adaptability ensures relevance and effectiveness, allowing individuals to capitalize on evolving opportunities and respond to emerging challenges with agility.

Mindfulness and emotional intelligence practices significantly enhance the evaluation process by promoting greater self-awareness and emotional resilience. Mindfulness techniques such as meditation encourage presence and reflection, offering clarity in understanding personal emotions and motivations. Practicing active listening and engaging in empathetic conversations deepen relationships and foster emotional intelligence, enriching the foundation upon which personal growth is built.

The evaluation of progress is more than a procedural task; it is a transformative opportunity to celebrate achievements, learn from setbacks, and recommit to personal visions. It encourages a mindset oriented towards growth and development, where each success serves as a stepping stone to future aspirations.

Embracing this mindset cultivates an inner resilience that empowers individuals to navigate challenges with grace and adaptability.

Incorporating regular evaluation into one's personal growth journey encourages a proactive stance towards life changes. By fostering a culture of reflection and feedback, individuals create a fertile environment for transformational growth, where insights and lessons learned inform future action. This iterative process shapes an evolving narrative of self-discovery and empowerment, propelling individuals towards a more fulfilling and enriched life.

Progress evaluation supports the conscious cultivation of a life aligned with personal values, aspirations, and strengths. By integrating these strategies and principles, individuals can effectively sustain their personal growth journey, navigating life's complexities with confidence and intention.

The ongoing practice of evaluating progress serves as a guidepost, ensuring that the journey towards personal empowerment remains both purposeful and rewarding for you.

Celebrating Your Successes

Celebrating your successes is an essential practice in sustaining personal growth and empowerment. This act of recognition acknowledges both the monumental and minute achievements along your journey, each contributing to building confidence, enhancing resilience, and solidifying motivation. The significance of celebration extends beyond personal validation; it creates an environment conducive to growth by reinforcing achievements and fostering a positive mindset.

Recognizing your successes serves as a catalyst for increased confidence and resilience, qualities that are crucial for facing life's inevitable challenges. Celebrating victories, no matter how small, provides a psychological boost that strengthens your ability to navigate adversity with motivation and determination. This boost is critical when confronting obstacles, as it imbues a sense of competence and preparedness to tackle future hurdles.

Success celebrations contribute to gaining clarity on what strategies and actions yield positive results.

By acknowledging achievements, you gain insights into effective practices and behaviors that can be replicated or adapted for continued success. This clarity informs decision-making in both personal and professional contexts, guiding future actions and aligning them with proven strategies. It creates a feedback loop where understanding what works well leads to refined approaches and sustained progress.

The importance of celebration is further underscored by its role in fostering a growth mindset. By focusing on successes rather than deficits, you nurture an appreciation for effort and progress. This mindset encourages learning from every experience, amplifying personal development and growth potential. Celebrating successes helps mitigate the inclination to dwell on negatives, promoting a balanced perspective that recognizes effort and triumph as integral parts of the growth process.

Incorporating celebrations into daily life strengthens relationships and builds a supportive community. Recognizing achievements within teams or social circles fosters a culture where everyone feels valued and motivated. This collective acknowledgment enhances morale and encourages collaboration, as members are inspired by shared successes. A positive support network emerges, characterized by mutual respect and encouragement, vital for nurturing long-lasting relationships and community ties.

Practical strategies can enhance the effectiveness of celebrating successes. Practicing gratitude daily imbues life with a sense of positivity and appreciation, setting a fertile ground for recognizing achievements. This practice involves reflecting on things for which you are thankful, reinforcing an appreciative mindset. achievable goals Setting provides specific, frequent opportunities for celebration. Breaking down larger objectives into manageable tasks ensures that milestones are recognized regularly, maintaining momentum and highlighting progress along the way.

Documenting your progress is another powerful tool in celebrating successes. Keeping a record of achievements serves as a source of motivation and reflection, showcasing the distance traversed since the beginning of your journey. This documentation can take various forms, such as journaling or maintaining a digital record of milestones, each entry a testament to growth and effort. Reviewing past achievements not only motivates but also provides a repository of learning moments and insights that can guide future endeavors.

Celebrating successes has a profound impact on personal growth by establishing a positive reinforcement cycle. Recognizing accomplishments reinforces the behaviors and methods that led to success, creating a foundation for continued achievement. It enhances your ability to tune into opportunities, bolstering confidence in your capabilities and encouraging you to pursue new challenges and experiences. When times become challenging, recalling and celebrating past successes provides the resilience and motivation needed to persevere and overcome obstacles.

The transformative power of celebrating successes lies in its ability to drive sustained personal growth and empowerment. It transforms the act of attaining goals into a journey rich with reflection and discovery, where each success contributes to a tapestry of achievement. This practice builds a mindset oriented toward possibilities and growth, infusing daily experiences with joy and purpose.

Through this celebration, personal and collective growth become tangible, where past achievements illuminate potential, and future possibilities beckon with promise. Celebrating successes not only sustains motivation but also deepens the understanding of personal strengths and capabilities. It fosters an environment where individuals are encouraged to explore, learn, and grow beyond perceived limits.

Ultimately, the practice of celebrating successes is an ongoing commitment to recognizing the value of each step in your journey. It invites a continuous exploration of growth, characterized by gratitude, reflection, and resilience. This commitment empowers individuals to navigate life's complexities with optimism, insight, and courage, strengthening their inner force and forging a path to a more empowered and fulfilling life.

CHAPTER 11: Sharing Your Authentic Story

The Power of Vulnerability

The power of vulnerability resides at the heart of genuine human connection and personal empowerment. Contrary to societal notions that equate vulnerability with weakness, embracing and expressing one's vulnerabilities can be an unparalleled source of strength. It is a transformative tool that facilitates self-discovery and fosters deeper relationships with others. By acknowledging and sharing our imperfections and fears, we cultivate an environment where authenticity thrives, enabling personal growth and empathy.

Courage serves as the foundation of vulnerability. This courage is not characterized by the absence of fear but by the willingness to be open and imperfect. It involves the deliberate choice to present oneself openly, exposing emotions and thoughts that are often hidden behind a facade of invulnerability. This courageous act creates a platform for genuine interaction, where others are invited to witness and understand our true selves. By embracing this courage, individuals dismantle the barriers that shield their authentic selves, paving the way for meaningful connections.

Alongside courage, vulnerability requires the practice of compassion, both towards oneself and others. Self-compassion involves extending kindness and understanding in the face of personal shortcomings, recognizing that imperfection is inherent to the human condition. This acceptance fosters a nurturing internal dialogue that encourages growth rather than self-criticism. By embracing compassion, individuals learn to accept their vulnerabilities without judgment, creating a more balanced perspective that honors both strengths and weaknesses.

The potential for connection is a profound benefit of vulnerability. Authentic interactions rooted in vulnerability foster trust and intimacy, laying the groundwork for deeper and more meaningful relationships. When individuals share their true selves, including fears and doubts, they break down the walls of pretense and invite genuine connections. This openness cultivates an environment where shared experiences and emotions bind people together, reinforcing bonds and enhancing mutual support. Vulnerability creates a space where empathy and understanding flourish, leading to a sense of belonging and shared humanity.

Acceptance is the final piece of the vulnerability puzzle; it means embracing one's vulnerabilities and imperfections as natural facets of existence. This acceptance is a liberating practice that dispels the fear of judgment and rejection, empowering individuals to step into their authentic selves. By acknowledging vulnerabilities, individuals affirm their humanity and demonstrate to others that flaws are not deficiencies but integral components of an authentic life. This acceptance is transformative, fostering resilience and integrating vulnerability as a recognized element of personal identity.

Vulnerability is particularly potent in the journey of personal empowerment. Sharing one's authentic story, enriched with its unique fears, doubts, and weaknesses, becomes a testament to the power of vulnerability. By stepping into this space of openness, individuals harness vulnerability as a tool for self-discovery and empowerment. This act of sharing breaks down internal and external barriers, fostering a communal sense of support and understanding. It encourages others to also express their true selves, creating a ripple effect that broadens the scope for personal and collective growth.

As individuals embrace vulnerability, they find themselves overcoming the fear of judgment and rejection. The realization that vulnerability is a universal experience bridges the gap between perceived isolation and community. By allowing oneself to be seen and understood, individuals dismantle the power of fear, transforming it into a source of empowerment. This shift leads to personal growth, as each moment of vulnerability becomes a step towards a more authentic and fulfilling life.

This act of opening up and being genuine is distinct from exposing oneself to harm; rather, it is an act of personal courage that seeks to achieve greater self-awareness and deeper emotional connections. Vulnerability becomes a bridge that connects individuals with their inner selves and with others, enhancing empathy and creating an environment conducive to solidarity and strength.

In summary, vulnerability is a transformative force with the power to enhance personal growth and foster meaningful relationships. By embracing vulnerability, individuals cultivate courage, compassion, acceptance, connection, transforming and perceived weaknesses into profound strengths. This practice of vulnerability empowers individuals to live authentically, guiding them toward a life enriched by deeper connections and self-understanding. Embracing the power of vulnerability promises not only personal growth but also a shared journey towards more profound human connection and empowerment.

Creating a Personal Narrative

Creating a personal narrative is a powerful exercise in self-exploration and empowerment, allowing individuals to articulate their journeys in ways that resonate and inspire. A well-crafted personal narrative does more than convey a series of events; it crafts a tapestry of experiences that reveal insights into who you are and how you have evolved. By structuring your narrative thoughtfully and authentically, you invite readers into your world, offering them a glimpse of your inner landscape and the transformative lessons you've learned along the way.

The foundation of a compelling personal narrative lies in a clear structure or outline. Structuring your story involves organizing it into coherent parts that form a logical flow from introduction to conclusion. This clarity in structure helps anchor your narrative, ensuring that each section contributes to the overarching theme or moral you aim to convey. Begin by defining the key moments of your journey—those pivotal experiences that have shaped your path. Organize these events in a sequence that reflects your growth, allowing the story to unfold naturally and with purpose.

Writing in the first person brings an intimate touch to your narrative, establishing a direct connection with your reader. Using "*I*" enables readers to step into your shoes, experiencing your story through your perspective. This personal approach fosters empathy and engagement but requires careful balance to avoid repetitive language. Varying sentence structure and integrating other narrative techniques ensures that the language remains dynamic and engaging, inviting readers to invest emotionally in your journey.

Engaging storytelling is essential for capturing and holding your audience's attention. Begin with a vivid scene or an emotional moment that draws readers into the narrative from the outset. Whether it's a challenging encounter, a moment of triumph, or a serene reflection, this initial hook sets the stage, providing a sensory entry point into your story. Use techniques like showing instead of telling to paint vivid pictures of settings and characters, allowing readers to see, feel, and experience the unfolding narrative.

Chronological order is a practical approach that aids in conveying your story with clarity and coherence. Sequencing events in the order they occurred helps maintain a clear timeline, ensuring readers can easily follow the evolution of your journey. This structure helps incorporate all significant incidents that have contributed to your personal growth and self-discovery, guiding readers through the narrative with an intuitive understanding of its progression.

Detailed and vivid descriptions enrich your narrative, bringing it to life with color and texture. Describing characters, settings, and pivotal events with depth prompts readers to visualize and engage fully with your story. Subplots and interesting developments add layers of intrigue, keeping readers captivated and invested in your journey. These elements not only enhance storytelling but also contextualize your experiences, providing a fuller picture of the influences that have shaped you.

The process of editing and proofreading cannot be overstated in crafting a polished narrative. After drafting your story, rigorously revise your work to refine clarity and precision. Eliminating repetitions, rephrasing awkward sentences, and correcting grammatical or spelling errors uphold the professionalism and readability of your narrative.

This diligence in editing ensures the final product is not only engaging but also a true reflection of your insights and experiences.

Authenticity forms the heart of a personal narrative. Sharing your genuine experiences, emotions, and thoughts creates a powerful emotional connection with your readers. As you narrate your journey of self-discovery and empowerment, it is this honesty that allows others to see reflections of their struggles and victories in your story. This connection fosters inspiration, compelling readers to reflect on their own paths and consider the transformative possibilities within their journeys.

Focusing on authenticity necessitates courage, as it often involves revealing vulnerabilities and admitting imperfections. Yet it is within these honest portrayals that the power of storytelling lies, as readers are drawn to narratives that resonate with truth and humanity. Embracing this vulnerability not only enriches your story but also empowers both you and your audience with the realization that personal growth is a process shared by all.

As you craft your personal narrative, remember that it is uniquely yours—a distinct composition shaped by your experiences, reflections, and aspirations.

It serves as a testament to your resilience, wisdom, and transformation, offering insights and encouragement to those who read it. By sharing your authentic story, you contribute to a collective tapestry of human experience, one where individual journeys weave into the broader narrative of empowerment and discovery.

Incorporating these aspects into your personal narrative culminates in a compelling story that resonates deeply with readers. It honors your journey, celebrates your growth, and inspires others by illustrating the power of vulnerability and authenticity in the pursuit of self-understanding and empowerment. This narrative becomes a beacon for both you and your audience, illuminating paths to deeper connection and shared humanity.

Inspiring Others Through Your Journey

The power of sharing one's journey lies in its capacity to inspire and connect, serving as a beacon for others navigating their own paths of growth and transformation. By recounting personal experiences, including both triumphs and challenges, individuals can provide invaluable insights into the process of personal development. This storytelling not only showcases resilience and success but also demystifies the incremental nature of growth, highlighting that achievements are often the culmination of ongoing perseverance and dedication rather than instant outcomes.

Authentic storytelling is one of the most potent tools for building empathy and connection. When individuals share their vulnerabilities alongside their successes, they resonate with others on a profound level. This honesty in communication helps to dissolve the isolation many feel in their struggles, reassuring them that they are not alone. The shared experiences foster a sense of community, where others can find strength and motivation, spurred by the realization that obstacles can be overcome and that personal aspirations are attainable.

Inspiring others through personal narrative involves embodying leadership qualities such as integrity, enthusiasm, and attentive listening. True leaders motivate by demonstrating passion and commitment to their values and goals, which naturally fosters motivation and collaboration within a group. By openly sharing their stories and the lessons learned along the way, leaders model a growth mindset that encourages others to challenge themselves and pursue their goals. This approach not only inspires others but facilitates the leader's own continuous self-discovery and growth.

Effective communication stands at the core of inspiring others. Techniques such as sharing knowledge generously, maintaining a positive attitude, and expressing gratitude can cultivate a nurturing and motivational environment. Clear, empathetic communication fosters trust, inviting others to share their aspirations and supporting them in their endeavors. This mutual exchange amplifies personal influence and reinforces a culture where personal and collective aspirations are supported and pursued together.

The act of sharing one's journey is as enriching for the storyteller as it is for the audience. Reflecting on personal experiences and one's articulating them to others reveals new insights into strengths and areas for improvement. This reflective process enhances self-awareness, offering clarity about personal values and motivations. It can further motivate individuals to remain committed to their own path of personal empowerment and discovery, constantly evolving and adapting in the pursuit of self-fulfillment.

The impact of sharing an authentic story extends beyond immediate interactions, creating a ripple effect that influences a broader community. As individuals draw inspiration and strength from these narratives, they carry forward the encouragement and motivation, affecting those around them. This ripple effect gradually cultivates a culture of support, continuous improvement, and shared empowerment. The inspiration passed from one to another creates a chain reaction, where each link in the chain becomes a source of further influence and transformation.

The power of inspiring others through personal storytelling lies in the authenticity and relatability of the narrative. When people hear about real challenges and authentic triumphs, they understand that growth is a universal journey and feel empowered to embark on their own paths. Sharing stories breaks barriers and encourages a diverse expression of experiences, reinforcing that there are many ways to pursue and achieve personal growth.

In summary, the art of sharing an authentic journey is transformative, both for the storyteller and the audience. It bridges the gap between personal experience and communal empowerment, paving the way for collective growth and understanding. By embracing and sharing personal narratives, individuals contribute to a larger movement of empowerment and self-discovery, inspiring others to explore their potential and embrace their own transformative paths. Through this continuous exchange of stories and insights, a tapestry of human experience is woven, one where every individual's journey is a thread that adds richness and depth to a shared pursuit of growth and fulfillment.

CHAPTER 12: Embracing Change and New Beginnings

Rituals for Transition

Rituals in modern life are experiencing a renaissance as essential tools for resilience and meaning-making amidst the pressures of rapid change. These practices are shedding their perception as mere traditional relics, evolving into powerful frameworks that facilitate personal and collective transitions. In an era characterized by digital saturation and post-pandemic recalibrations, rituals offer a grounded approach to managing complexity and fostering emotional well-being.

Rituals are being embraced for their capacity to guide individuals and communities through pivotal life changes. Whether navigating career transitions, undergoing personal growth journeys, or experiencing collective mourning, rituals provide a structured way to reflect on past experiences while envisioning future possibilities. These practices create a pause in the flow of life, allowing individuals to process emotions, gain clarity, and renew their sense of purpose.

Beyond offering emotional resilience, rituals contribute to a sense of cohesion and belonging, especially in environments where teams are remote or fragmented. By fostering connection and a shared sense of ritual, workplaces can cultivate an atmosphere of trust and mutual support, critical components for team effectiveness. Rituals can take the form of small daily practices or larger communal events that bring people together in shared intention and support.

Modern iterations of rituals emphasize inclusivity and adaptability, catering to the diverse tapestry of genders, races, identities, and socioeconomic backgrounds. These rituals are crafted to reflect both traditional roots and contemporary needs, allowing individuals to engage in meaningful practices that resonate personally and communally. The integration of ancient wisdom with modern sensibilities creates rituals that are both grounded and versatile, meeting participants where they are.

The intersection of technology and spirituality is further transforming ritual practices. With the advent of AI-driven tools, new ritual languages are emerging, blending traditional ceremonies with digital elements to address post-pandemic grief and help individuals navigate transitions on multiple levels. This hybrid approach offers a unique opportunity to engage with spiritual practices in both offline and online contexts, enhancing accessibility and relevance.

Everyday acts are being reframed as sacred rituals, emphasizing the power of mindfulness and intention in daily routines. Simple practices such as starting the day with gratitude, engaging in meditation, or journaling are becoming integral elements of holistic self-care and personal growth. These rituals transform ordinary moments into expressions of sacredness and mindfulness, reinforcing the importance of living with intention and presence.

Rituals are inherently communal, designed to be shared experiences that provide strength and support during times of transition. Workshops and guided programs, like those led by individuals like Day Schildkret, create environments where participants can collaboratively forge modern rituals. These shared experiences support individuals in traversing life's changes with skill and grace, reaffirming the communal spirit essential for personal empowerment and collective resilience.

By acknowledging and integrating the renewed role rituals, individuals embrace a transformative tool for personal empowerment and self-discovery. Rituals offer not only a means of navigating life's transitions with greater ease but also encourage profound connections with one's inner self and the larger community. They invite participants to embrace the sacred in the everyday, reshaping moments of change as opportunities for growth and alignment with deeper purposes.

As rituals continue to evolve, they reflect a dynamic adaptability that honors both historical traditions and contemporary innovations. This fluidity ensures that rituals remain relevant, supporting diverse needs and fostering an inclusive sense of belonging and healing.

They serve as tangible reminders of the interconnectedness of life, offering pathways to navigate change that honor the past while embracing the future.

Ultimately, rituals inspire transformation by anchoring individuals in times of change, connecting them to community and their own inner wisdom. By incorporating rituals into lives marked by transition, individuals engage with their journey more mindfully, opening pathways for empowerment, resilience, and discovery. Through the intentional integration of ritual, life is imbued with meaning, guiding participants along their personal and shared narratives with clarity and purpose.

Letting Go of the Past

Letting go of the past emerges as a pivotal step in the journey towards personal growth and the embrace of new beginnings. It serves as both an emotional release and a conscious commitment to liberate oneself from the shackles of previous grievances, traumas, and negative experiences.

Holding onto the past can hinder one's ability to fully engage in the present and embrace future possibilities, creating a landscape where personal and mental well-being are compromised.

The psychological importance of letting go cannot be overstated. Persistent focus on past disappointments and resentments can cultivate a mental landscape dominated by stress and negativity, obstructing the path to emotional clarity and fulfillment. By consciously setting aside these weights, individuals open themselves up to growth, healing, and happiness. This act of release facilitates a more present-focused mindset, allowing life to be experienced as a dynamic process rich with potential.

Research underscores the profound benefits associated with letting go, particularly through the practice of forgiveness. Studies indicate that forgiveness plays a crucial role in alleviating mental health issues such as anxiety and depression. This psychological shift not only enhances emotional resilience but also mitigates the impact of stress accumulated over a lifetime.

The act of forgiving, whether it involves others or oneself, serves as a powerful catalyst for psychological liberation and renewal.

Forgiveness is a complex and multifaceted process. Distinguishing between forgiving others and oneself is essential, as individuals often grapple more intensely with self-forgiveness. Guilt and shame, arising from perceived personal failures or wrongdoings, can be more persistent and insidious than resentment toward others. Self-compassion, therefore, becomes essential in this healing process. By fostering self-compassion, individuals can address these destructive emotions, paving the way for internal peace and acceptance.

Embracing mindfulness and psychological flexibility enriches the process of letting go. Mindfulness encourages individuals to be present, fostering awareness and acceptance of emotions without judgment. This practice, alongside psychological flexibility, cultivates an adaptable mindset that embraces change and reduces attachment to unproductive thoughts or memories. Rooted in ancient philosophies such as Daoism and Buddhism, these practices invite a non-attached mindset that encourages the release of emotional burdens.

Cultural and personal nuances further shape the process of forgiveness and letting go. Different cultural contexts influence perceptions of forgiveness, affecting how individuals can reconcile personal healing with relational or systemic dynamics. It is vital for each person to articulate their interpretation of forgiveness, whether it serves to heal personal wounds, mend relationships, or address broader societal issues. Clarifying these aspects can guide individuals through the nuanced process of letting go with greater clarity and purpose.

Understanding the complexity of emotions linked to past relationships or experiences illuminates the transitional journey of letting go. The emotional bond with past events, despite their painful nature, signifies the importance they once held in shaping identity and perspective. Recognizing the science behind these attachments allows individuals to navigate the processes involved with insight and empathy. Letting go becomes a gentle unraveling of ties that no longer serve, but honor what once was, integrating lessons into the fabric of personal growth.

Time is a crucial dimension in the journey of letting go. Unlike physical actions, emotional release does not occur instantaneously. It unfolds as a gradual process, requiring patience and understanding. Appreciating this timeline, individuals can cultivate compassion toward their journey, allowing feelings and insights to emerge naturally, facilitating a deeper integration with current aspirations.

The impact on well-being from letting go of the past is transformative. This surrender of old grievances nurtures a state of well-being where present and future happiness can flourish. Through this liberation, individuals gain the freedom to make wiser choices, engage in healthier behaviors, and immerse themselves fully in present experiences. Living in the present moment enhances relationships, creativity, and satisfaction, underpinning the journey with vibrancy and positivity.

Letting go of the past is a courageous act of self-empowerment. By releasing the grip of bygone experiences, individuals reclaim narrative control, defining their identity not by past scars but by present strengths and future possibilities. It marks a transformative step in personal empowerment, where the potential for self-discovery becomes vast and invigorating. This practice continually unveils new facets of strength and resilience, emphasizing the power of personal transformation in the path to self-discovery and empowerment. Through letting go, individuals find the tranquility needed to embrace the uncharted paths of the future, guided by the inner force of renewal and resilience.

Welcoming Future Opportunities

Welcoming future opportunities requires an open heart and mind, ready to embrace the endless potential that lies ahead. In an ever-evolving world, the ability to adapt and grow is paramount, marking the difference between those who merely survive and those who thrive. This readiness for opportunities is underpinned by embracing a lifelong learning mindset—an attitude that places continuous education and personal growth at the forefront. Through formal education, online courses, workshops, and individuals self-directed cultivate learning, curiosity, open-mindedness, and adaptability. This mindset not only broadens intellectual horizons but also enhances the capacity to navigate new ideas, ensuring that individuals remain agile in adapting to the dynamic shifts of the modern world.

Adaptability and resilience are essential in a world characterized by rapid change. Embracing these qualities involves developing a robust change response system, fostering a growth mindset that perceives failures not as definitive setbacks but as invaluable learning experiences. By reframing failures as opportunities for growth, individuals build resilience, equipping themselves to handle the inevitable challenges of life with creativity and confidence. This resilient outlook encourages a proactive stance, empowering individuals to seize new opportunities with enthusiasm and determination.

The integration of technology and human-centric growth shapes the landscape of future opportunities. As digital skills become increasingly vital, proficiency in areas like AI literacy and data-driven methodologies can significantly enhance career trajectories and personal development. However, while embracing digital tools, it is crucial to maintain a balance with human-centric growth. Emotional intelligence and well-being are indispensable in the digital age, ensuring that technological advancements are met with an equal commitment to mental and emotional health. These dual focuses enhance both professional capabilities and personal satisfaction, fortifying the foundation upon which future opportunities rest.

Focusing on mental health and well-being is more critical now than ever. The expansion of therapy options, mindfulness apps, and wellness programs reflects a growing awareness that mental health is fundamental to personal and professional success.

Prioritizing self-care and resilience-building practices helps individuals manage stress and maintain balance, laying the groundwork for embracing new ventures with vigor. Mental well-being underpins effective decision-making and interpersonal relationships, critical elements in navigating new opportunities.

The landscape of self-improvement offers fertile ground for setting new goals and embarking on journeys of personal growth. The advent of *2025* stands as an invitation to adopt healthier habits, acquire new skills, and tackle projects that have long been postponed. It is a time ripe for reinvention, providing a chance to realign one's life with core values and aspirations. This alignment ensures that future pursuits are not only ambitious but deeply resonant with individual purpose, fostering fulfillment and empowerment.

Advances in education and learning break traditional barriers, making lifelong learning more accessible than ever. Online platforms and virtual certifications offer diverse opportunities for development, education facilitating and skill continuous improvement regardless of location or time constraints. These advancements democratize learning, leveling the playing field and allowing more individuals to capitalize on educational resources that support personal and professional aspirations. In this environment, knowledge becomes a practical tool for empowerment, a stepping stone toward realizing potential and achieving dreams.

Welcoming future opportunities involves weaving a tapestry of learning, adaptation, and personal growth. This approach embraces the interplay of technology with personal development, mental resilience with digital acumen, crafting a holistic strategy for thriving in a complex world. When these elements coalesce, individuals are well-prepared not only to navigate change but to pioneer new paths and initiatives.

By engaging with these opportunities, individuals align themselves with an evolving narrative of empowerment and discovery. They become architects of their futures, capable of designing lives enriched with purpose and innovation. These opportunities act as gateways, unlocking potential and inviting exploration into the depths of personal and professional capacities. As individuals embrace these possibilities, they ignite a force within that propels them toward success and self-realization, embodying the essence of transformation and forward momentum.

The key to embracing future opportunities lies in an unwavering commitment to growth, adaptation, and well-being. As the world continues to shift, those who can harness these principles will find themselves not merely responding to change but actively shaping it.

This proactive engagement with the future ensures a journey replete with discovery, fulfillment, and the enduring satisfaction of a life well-lived.

ACKNOWLEDGEMENT

I would like to express my heartfelt gratitude to the many individuals who have supported the creation of this book. The encouragement has been invaluable throughout this journey which has profoundly shaped my thinking and approach to writing in all.

Their wisdom and knowledge have been instrumental in my personal and professional growth which provided valuable insights, suggestions, and encouragement. Your belief in my vision gave me the confidence to share this story with the world.

And to my readers: your interest and support are the reasons this book exists. I hope it resonates with you and brings you as much joy in reading as it did for me in writing.

With deepest appreciation,

Dr. A. Romani

BIOGRAPHY

Dr. A. Romani is an indie author and inspirational storyteller who's made waves in the literary world with his unique voice and compelling narratives. Armed with a doctorate that sharpened his research and communication skills, he's built a diverse portfolio spanning multiple genres—each infused with his signature blend of inspiration and insight. What sets **Dr. Romani** apart is his commitment to the transformative power of stories. He doesn't just put books out there; he creates movements of positivity and encouragement. Through his Indie Author works, he connects directly with readers seeking both entertainment and enlightenment. His books consistently resonate with audiences worldwide, offering comfort and motivation to those navigating their own life stories. **Dr. Romani** believes every story has the potential to change lives, and he's dedicated to being that beacon of hope— one book, one story at a time.

www.ingramcontent.com/pod-product-compliance
Lightning Source LLC
LaVergne TN
LVHW090943080826
845145LV00003B/875